GW00381935

HEADLINE BRITONS

1926-1930

HEADLINE BRITONS

1926–1930

SEEN THROUGH SEVEN UNIQUE FIGURES OF THE TIME

PETER PUGH

Published in the UK in 2017 by
Icon Books Ltd, Omnibus Business Centre,
39–41 North Road, London N7 9DP
email: info@iconbooks.com
www.iconbooks.com

Sold in the UK, Europe and Asia
by Faber & Faber Ltd, Bloomsbury House,
74–77 Great Russell Street,
London WC1B 3DA or their agents

Distributed in the UK, Europe and Asia
by Grantham Book Services, Trent Road,
Grantham NG31 7XQ

Distributed in Australia and New Zealand
by Allen & Unwin Pty Ltd,
PO Box 8500, 83 Alexander Street,
Crows Nest, NSW 2065

Distributed in South Africa by
Jonathan Ball, Office B4, The District,
41 Sir Lowry Road, Woodstock 7925

Distributed in India by Penguin Books India,
7th Floor, Infinity Tower – C, DLF Cyber City,
Gurgaon 122002, Haryana

Distributed in Canada by Publishers Group Canada,
76 Stafford Street, Unit 300, Toronto, Ontario M6J 2S1

Distributed in the USA by Publishers Group West,
1700 Fourth Street, Berkeley, CA 94710

ISBN: 978-178578-210-7

Typeset and designed by Simmons Pugh

Printed and bound in the UK by Clays Ltd, St Ives plc

CONTENTS

ABOUT THE AUTHOR

Peter Pugh is a businessperson and company historian who has written more than 50 company histories on businesses from Rolls-Royce to Iceland. He is also the author of *Introducing Thatcherism* and *Introducing Keynes,* and lives by the sea in north Norfolk, and in Cambridge.

INTRODUCTION

E very publishing season sees the launch of books on famous characters of the twentieth century and many high achievers have more than one book about them. For example, the number of books on Winston Churchill is in the twenties or thirties and recently there was another book on Clement Attlee.

This new series Icon is launching will cover the last 100 years of British history in five-year splits – the first two are 1921–25 and 1926–30 and, as well as giving the background, both social and economic, of those years, will concentrate on the interesting and often misunderstood characters that featured in them.

One of the main characters in this second book, 1926–30, is Radclyffe Hall, the lesbian author who wrote books about homosexuality at a time when it was still frowned upon and indeed was illegal. Also featured is the famous inventor of television, John Logie Baird. Then there is the founder of the first mass-market motor car, William Morris, later Lord Nuffield, as well as the modernist writer Virginia Woolf. Staying with the world of the arts, we shall also discuss the playwright, novelist and short story writer Somerset Maugham, as well as the famous wit, playwright, composer and actor Noël Coward. In addition, Ramsay MacDonald, the first Labour prime minister, was a prominent figure during these years.

MONETARY VALUES

Money and its value is always a problem when writing about a period that stretches over a number of years. Furthermore, establishing a yardstick for measuring the change in the value of money is not easy either. Do we take the external value of the £ or what it will buy in the average (whatever that may be) weekly shopping basket? Do we relate it to the average manual wage? As we know, while prices in general might rise, and have done so in this country every year since the Second World War, the prices of certain products might fall. However, we have to make some judgements. We can only generalise, and I think the best yardstick is probably the average working wage.

Taking this as the yardstick, here is a measure of the £ sterling relative to the £ in 2017.

Apart from wartime, prices were stable for 250 years, but prices began to rise in the run-up to the First World War.

1665–1900 multiply by 120
1900–1914 multiply by 110
1918–39 multiply by 60
1945–50 multiply by 35
1950–60 multiply by 30
1960–70 multiply by 25
1970–74 multiply by 20

1975–77 multiply by 15
1978–80 multiply by 8
1980–87 multiply by 5
1987–91 multiply by 2.5
1991–97 multiply by 2
1997–2010 multiply by 1.5

Since 2010, the rate of inflation, by the standards of most of the twentieth century, has been very low, averaging, until very recently, less than the 1997–2010 Labour government's originally stated aim of 2.5 per cent (since reduced to 2 per cent). You don't need me to tell you that some things such as telephone charges and many items made in the Far East, notably China, can go down in price while others, such as houses, have moved up very sharply from 1997 to 2017.

TIMELINE FOR 1926–30

- 1926 -

April   The Duchess of York gives birth to a daughter, Princess Elizabeth

May   A General Strike in support of mine workers is declared. It is the first such strike in British history. It collapses nine days later. Only the miners continue the fight

     Rudolph Valentino dies suddenly of peritonitis

August   England wins the Ashes for the first time in fourteen years, beating Australia by 289 runs in the fifth Test

November   An Imperial conference announces that Canada, Australia, New Zealand, South Africa and Newfoundland are to have dominion status. They will be self-governing, and will have equal standing with Britain within the Commonwealth

Books
Seven Pillars of Wisdom by T.E. Lawrence
Winnie-the-Pooh by A.A. Milne

Films

Ben Hur starring Ramon Novarro (released December
   1925 but became popular in 1926)
Don Juan starring John Barrymore
The General starring Buster Keaton

- 1927 -

January   It becomes possible to telephone New York
from London at a cost of £15 (£900 in today's
money) for three minutes

May   Charles Lindbergh arrives in Paris after taking
33½ hours to fly solo from New York

November   In the first London-to-Brighton car rally John
Bryce's car is registered as competitor Number 1
Joseph Stalin expels Leon Trotsky and other
opponents from the Soviet Communist party

Books

Tarka the Otter by Henry Williamson
To the Lighthouse by Virginia Woolf

Films

The Jazz Singer
The Kid Brother starring Harold Lloyd
Flesh and the Devil starring Greta Garbo

- 1928 -

March   The voting age for women is lowered to 21. Now women have the same voting rights as men

May   The Bank of England plans to issue £1 and 10s notes, in addition to the £5 banknotes and larger denominations which are already in circulation

September   Alexander Fleming discovers penicillin

October   The Soviet Union's first five-year plan begins. From now on, all factories and farms work to fulfil 'norms' of production handed down by the state

November   Hirohito is crowned Emperor of Japan

Books
Lady Chatterley's Lover by D.H. Lawrence
Orlando by Virginia Woolf

Films
Steamboat Willie, the first Mickey Mouse cartoon
Two Tars starring Stan Laurel and Oliver Hardy

- 1929 -

March   A record 66 runners compete in the Grand National at Aintree

June   A Labour government comes to power under
            Ramsay MacDonald
            Margaret Bondfield, minister of labour, is the
            first female Cabinet member

October   The New York Stock Exchange crashes

Books
Goodbye to All That by Robert Graves
A Farewell to Arms by Ernest Hemingway

Films
Big Business starring Laurel and Hardy
Bulldog Drummond

- 1930 -

March   Gandhi tells British Viceroy of India to expect
            civil disobedience

July   Donald Bradman scores record 309 runs in a
            day

September   National Socialists win 107 seats in German
            Parliament

Books
Murder at the Vicarage by Agatha Christie
Swallows and Amazons by Arthur Ransome

Films

Abraham Lincoln
All Quiet on the Western Front
Journey's End

TIMELINE FOR THE BBC

- 1926 -

4 May   The General Strike begins. The BBC broadcasts five news bulletins a day as no newspapers are published

- 1927 -

1 January   The British Broadcasting Company becomes the British Broadcasting Corporation when it is granted a royal charter. Sir John Reith becomes the first director general

15 January   First live sports broadcast on the BBC. The rugby union England vs Wales match is commentated on by Teddy Wakelam

22 January   First live football match broadcast, featuring Arsenal's home league fixture against Sheffield United at Highbury

January   First BBC reference library established by Florence Milnes

March   The BBC coat of arms is adopted

7 July   Christopher Stone presents a record programme, becoming the first British disc jockey

21 August   The first high-powered regional station (5GB), forerunner of the Midland Regional Programme, opens at Daventry

- 1929 -

20 August   First transmissions of John Logie Baird's experimental 30-line television system

- 1930 -

9 March   The majority of the BBC's existing radio stations are regrouped to form the BBC National Programme and the BBC Regional Programme

14 July   Transmission of the first experimental television play, *The Man With the Flower in His Mouth*

30 September

        Number of radio licences reaches 12 million, or roughly every second home in the country

LIST OF ILLUSTRATIONS

CHAPTER 1

THE GOLD STANDARD AND GENERAL STRIKE

In 1925 Winston Churchill, then chancellor of the exchequer, took Britain back on to the Gold Standard, the system whereby the pound was defined in terms of a fixed quantity of gold. He would personally have preferred not to. However, many of his advisers, including Montagu Norman, governor of the Bank of England, were in favour as was the Labour party and Churchill's prime minister, Stanley Baldwin.

In hindsight, the rate at which the currency was fixed was far too high as the pound was pegged back at its pre-war rate of $4.87 (for comparison, it is currently about $1.30). The effect was almost disastrous for many in British industry, especially those with strong exports. For example, in shipbuilding where unemployment was already at 30 per cent, more were laid off and in Barrow-in-Furness unemployment rose to 49 per cent.

This is what Boris Johnson wrote about Winston Churchill's responsibility for taking the pound back on to the Gold Standard in his book, *The Churchill Factor*:

It is widely agreed that Churchill's Chancellorship – whatever its merits – was blighted by wrongly 'Going Back on Gold' … and at the wrong rate. Everyone now accepts that this was a catastrophic error. The value of sterling was pegged back at its pre-war rate of $4.87 – which meant the pound was overvalued, with fatal consequences for British industry. Exports became too expensive to compete on world markets.

Businesses tried to cut costs by laying off staff or cutting wages. There were strikes, unemployment, chaos – and then the crash of 1929, and still no escape from the punishing regime of the Gold Standard.

In the end the pound was forced off gold in 1931 by a series of speculative attacks on the foreign exchange markets – just as it was prised out of the ERM (Exchange Rate Mechanism) in 1992. Churchill carried the can for the whole disaster, and John Maynard Keynes wrote a denunciation called *The Economic Consequences of Mr Churchill*. It was indeed his decision, and as Chancellor, he cannot escape the blame. [...]

The trouble was that he was surrounded by a lot of clever people who thought they knew about economics; and they thought the Gold Standard was a frightfully good idea. The most ineffably self-confident of them all was the Governor of the Bank of England, the nattily dressed Montagu Norman. 'I will make you the Golden Chancellor,' he told Churchill. But Norman was not alone in his delusions.

The City was for it; the Labour Party was for it; Stanley Baldwin himself thought it would be easier just to get on and do it. In the end Churchill held a famous dinner party at Number 11 Downing Street, on 17 March 1925, and invited Keynes to come and put the contrary point of view. Alas, Keynes had a cold and was off form. Churchill the gold-o-sceptic found himself outnumbered, and reluctantly conceded.

The point is that he went back on gold in spite of his better judgement – and his judgement was better than that of a whole host of supposed financial experts. For those who remember recent British monetary history, he was in exactly the same position as Mrs Thatcher when she was bamboozled (by Nigel Lawson and Geoffrey Howe) into joining the disastrous European Exchange Rate Mechanism in 1989.

And Simon Schama in his *A History of Britain* agreed that the return to the Gold Standard was a disaster:

> There was much trumpeting of the return of the great, solid, pound sterling and of the 'shackling' of the British economy to reality. But beyond the imperial fetishising of sterling, that reality as predicted by Henderson and Keynes, was shocking. The effect of a pound over-valued at $4.87 was to make the goods and services of the most labour-intensive industries even less competitive in export markets. Prices, and the number out of work, shot up; wages fell. In the worst-affected industries, like shipbuilding, unemployment was already approaching 30 per cent; in Barrow-in-Furness, indeed, it was a massive 49 per cent. The mine-owners' response to the deepening crisis, made even worse by the fact that the German coalfields were back in production, was to demand wage cuts and extensions to working hours. The unions, on the other hand, asked for wage increases and discounted coal prices.

The General Strike

1926 was the year of the General Strike: an attempt by the major unions, with the miners in the van, to resist attempts by employers to cut their wages. As we have seen, the strength of sterling and the consequent problem of an overvalued currency was exacerbated in 1925 when the chancellor of the exchequer, Winston Churchill, took Britain back on to the Gold Standard which had prevailed throughout the nineteenth century and up to the First World War. In the 1920s, the pre-war era was seen as a golden age (there certainly was not the equivalent feeling in the late 1940s after the Second World War, when no one saw the 1930s as a golden age), and many thought that if only the conditions of that time could be created again, all would be well. These conditions included a £ valued at nearly $5 and not the $3.60 that prevailed in the first half of the 1920s. However, conditions had changed, and reverting to such an exchange rate merely made Britain's competitive position even worse than it was already. For many employers the only answer was to cut wages. For many workers the only answer was to strike.

At the end of the nineteenth and the beginning of the twentieth centuries the working classes of a number of European countries, such as Belgium, Russia, Sweden and Germany, had organised general strikes. For example, Leon Trotsky, a key person in the Russian Revolution of 1917, wrote:

> The general strike is one of the most acute forms of class war. It is one step from the general strike to armed insurrection … If carried through to the end, the general strike brings the revolutionary class up against the task of organising a new state power … A real victory for the general strike can only be found in the conquest of power by the proletariat.

In the mid-1920s, there had been a number of successful strikes throughout Britain such as the Clydeside general strike for a 40-hour week in 1919 and the strike by 300,000 Lancashire cotton workers for a 30 per cent wage increase, and in addition wages were reduced in the slowdown of 1923 and 1924. Perhaps as a result of these conditions, a call for a general strike received widespread support.

Coal mining was the largest and most important industry in Britain and its union, the Miners' Federation of Great Britain (MFGB), was a major force in the trade union movement.

Coal production had declined sharply. Output per man had fallen to 199 tons in the early 1920s compared with 247 tons before the First World War and a peak of 310 tons in the 1880s. Mine owners were still keen to maintain their profits, and consequently put pressure on the miners by reducing their wages and increasing their hours. In the seven years up to 1926, miners' pay went down from £6 a week to £3.90 (£360 to £234 in today's money). King George V tried to calm things down and commented: 'Try living on their wages before you judge them.' The MFGB, saying: 'Not a penny off the pay, not a minute on the day', effectively led the trade union movement into a general strike.

This is what Roy Hattersley, a minister of the Labour government under Harold Wilson in the 1960s, wrote about the General Strike of 1926:

> The world was changing but Britain was slow to adapt and accommodate the change. The old industries – steel, coal and shipbuilding – were beginning to die and their death was felt most painfully by the poor. It was the miners – always the shock troops of the trade union army – who fought the valiant, and most obviously doomed, rearguard actions against reality. The leaders of the TUC knew that a strike in support of the old rates of pay and hours of work could not be won. And the coal owners were determined to starve the workers into submission. But it was neither betrayal nor brutality which beat the Miners' Federation. It was the passage of time.

Ramsay MacDonald, the leader of the Labour party, was against the General Strike from the start. But loyalty compelled him to give it his formal support. Solidarity with the working class is in fact not a virtue normally associated with MacDonald. He is condemned in Labour folklore as a traitor who deserted his party and led a 'national' government. But perhaps he was less a villain than a victim of the belief that only he could save the nation from financial disaster. Unhappily he had no idea how salvation could be achieved, and the authorities on economic survival feared to give him firm advice in case their prescription proved inadequate. He chose to do his duty as he saw it. This would ultimately require him to abandon both the party and the beliefs which had sustained him for 30 years.

Poverty was, of course, greatest in the areas where once the old industries had flourished. The middle class thrived, but families at the bottom of the income scale endured every sort of deprivation and, as the numerous marches to London discovered along the way, too few people cared. Among those that did were the churches. For the first time, the Church of England discovered its mission to urban Britain.

It was in housing that the Church's campaign was most effective. In towns and cities from London to Leeds the Church of England drew the nation's attention to the horror of life in the Victorian slums, and the government was stung into action. The encouragement of house building – in all its forms – was one of the few preoccupations for which the inter-war governments can take credit. It was about the only way in which the conditions in which the poor lived were improved.

As we have seen, the General Strike had many different causes, but the final trigger came in March 1926 when the

Royal Commission set up by prime minister Stanley Baldwin to look into the mining industry reported, recommending wage reductions for the miners. The miners appealed to the general council of the TUC, which called for a general strike. This, the General Strike of 1926, lasted nine days. Despite bitter feelings, it was remarkably peaceful. Both sides were firm but well-disciplined, and there were few ugly incidents. Volunteers who manned buses, trains and other essential services were assaulted vocally rather than physically. Workers' councils issued permits for essential supplies to be delivered. But the TUC leaders were divided. Some thought the strike might get out of hand, because extreme militants were gaining popularity. In the end, against the miners' wishes, the TUC agreed to end the strike in exchange for somewhat vague government promises. Since the strike had been going well, there was a natural feeling of betrayal among many strikers. The trade union movement was weakened, a fact reinforced in 1927 when the triumphant government introduced a Trade Disputes Act making general strikes and 'sympathetic' strikes illegal, and attacking Labour party finance. Trade union members would in future 'contract in' to pay the political contribution, which went to the Labour party, instead of 'contracting out' of the otherwise automatic payment of their contributions.

Churchill was one of the more vociferous and militant anti-union members of the government, although subsequently he did cooperate with the minister of health, Neville Chamberlain, in introducing new social welfare measures. These included a new Pensions Act, and a Local Government Act which transferred the old Poor Law guardians' work to local authorities. This Conservative government also extended state control in the generation of electricity; the

Central Electricity Board was set up, and soon there was a national electricity grid. The conversion of the British Broadcasting Company to the state British Broadcasting Corporation was also a nationalising measure even though the old company's managing director, Reith, stayed on.

Aftermath of the conflict

The miners remained on strike for some time but a continuing lack of money meant they needed to return to work and, by the end of November, most of them were indeed back down the mines. Others remained unemployed for years, while the ones who went back to work had to put up with longer hours, lower wages and local wage agreements. Those that had gone on strike became convinced they had achieved nothing at all.

And this had a great effect on the mining industry. By the late 1930s, employment in mining was down to only two-thirds of the 1.2 million it had been in the early 1920s. However, at the same time, productivity increased from under 200 tons per miner to over 300 tons by 1939.

In some mining areas, strike breakers were ostracised in their communities for the rest of their lives, and some were still being referred to as 'scabs' at the time of the 1984–85 strike.

CHAPTER 2

VIRGINIA WOOLF AND THE REJECTION OF CONVENTION

Born in 1882, Virginia Woolf was a significant contributor to the culture and society of the 1920s. Her parents, Sir Leslie and Julia Stephen, brought her up with a literary background and Virginia became a successful novelist herself. Her best-known titles were *Mrs Dalloway*, published in 1925, *To the Lighthouse*, 1927, and *Orlando*, 1928. She also wrote a book-length essay called *A Room of One's Own*, which was aimed at female students at Cambridge.

In this essay she wrote:

> May I remind you that most of the professions have been open to you for close on ten years now? ... There must at this moment be some 2,000 women capable of earning £500 (£30,000 in today's money) a year in one way or another, you will agree that the excuse of lack of opportunity, training, employment, leisure and money no longer holds good.

She was brought up in St Ives in Cornwall but eventually moved to Gordon Square in Bloomsbury. This was where she met Lytton Strachey, Clive Bell, Rupert Brooke, Duncan Grant, Leonard Woolf, John Maynard Keynes, David Garnett and Roger Fry with whom she founded the Bloomsbury Group, which became immensely influential.

In 1912 Virginia married the author Leonard Woolf. He was not wealthy and Virginia referred to him during their engagement as a 'penniless Jew'! Indeed, it is strange that Virginia did marry a Jewish man because much of her writing and behaviour suggests that she held anti-Semitic views. In her writing she often described Jews as physically repulsive and dirty. When she was on a cruise to Portugal there were 'a great many Portuguese Jews on board, and other repulsive objects, but we kept clear of them'. And she wrote in her diary: 'I do not like the Jewish voice; I do not like the Jewish laugh.' Later, however, she said: 'How I hated marrying a Jew – What a snob I was, for they have immense vitality.'

In 1917 the Woolfs founded the Hogarth Press. It was started with one hand press costing £19 or about £1,000 in today's money, but eventually published Virginia's novels as well as works by T.S. Eliot, Laurens van der Post and others. Eventually Hogarth Press became part of Random House which merged with Penguin in 2013 and is now part of the German Bertelsmann Group.

Vita Sackville-West, famous today primarily for the creation of the magnificent gardens at Sissinghurst Castle in Kent which were taken over by the National Trust in 1947, had married Harold Nicholson in 1913 and though they had two children, nevertheless they both had homosexual affairs.

Vita's longest relationship was with Violet Trefusis, which began shortly after they met when Vita was twelve and Violet ten. However, her best-known affair was with Virginia Woolf. Indeed it was her love for Vita that inspired Virginia to write *Orlando*, later described by Vita's son Nigel Nicolson, who wrote:

> The effect of Vita on Virginia is all contained in *Orlando*, the longest and most charming love letter in literature, in which she explores Vita, weaves her in and out of the centuries, tosses her from one sex to the other, plays with her, dresses her in furs, laces and emeralds, teases her, flirts with her, drops a veil of mist around her.

Orlando was published at about the same time as Radclyffe Hall's *The Well of Loneliness*. Hall was surprised that, as she had been prosecuted for obscenity, Virginia was not prosecuted as well. In her biography of Radclyffe Hall, Sally Cline tried to explain the reason:

> Orlando, who changes sex and lives through several centuries, is a female erotic who cannot be tied down, either by gender or by time. Rebecca West hailed *Orlando* as a beautiful exploration which turned a 'dark jungle into a safe habitation for the spirit'. If the dark jungle was antique male-dominated literary traditions or dark undiscovered places in psychology, then Woolf was set on the same course as Radclyffe Hall, who had plumbed dark places in *The Well*, and Djuna Barnes who was exploring new areas of the jungle on her way towards *Nightwood*. Hall, Barnes and Woolf were all venturing through hitherto unexplored territory within the male literary world.
>
> Radclyffe Hall must have puzzled at length as to why *Orlando* (like *Extraordinary Women*) did not come under the censor's ban. Called 'the longest and most charming love letter in literature', it was an overt Sapphic portrait which even included photographs of the author's lover. But the difference between Woolf's sexual presentations and Hall's was that although same-sex desire in the form of eroticized relationships between women is fundamental in Woolf's writings, it is always emotional, elusive, imaginary or symbolic.

Although both Radclyffe Hall and Virginia Woolf were lesbians and prepared to write books in support of women's love for each other, the difference was that Virginia felt her lesbianism was an emotional and sometimes sexual orientation rather than a political identity, whereas Radclyffe felt her 'inversion' was not only personal but also political.

CHAPTER 3

RADCLYFFE HALL – 'THAT NIGHT THEY WERE NOT DIVIDED'

Given her upbringing, perhaps it is not surprising that Radclyffe Hall was different from most other women of her time.

Christened Marguerite Radclyffe-Hall, she was born on 12 August 1880 at Sunny Lawn, Dudley Road, Bournemouth (which was then in Hampshire but is now in Dorset). Her father, Radclyffe Radclyffe-Hall, was something of a philanderer and her mother, Mary Jane Hall, had a reputation for being quarrelsome. Indeed, her father was nicknamed 'Rat' and saw his daughter only a few times before he and her mother were divorced. Her mother was not only quarrelsome but was also a bully and subjected Radclyffe to physical punishment. Furthermore, her stepfather later also beat her and possibly sexually abused her.

Sally Cline, who wrote a book about Radclyffe Hall, said:

> The psychological effects of abuse on her were extreme nervousness, outbursts of wild temper, feelings of restriction, fear of being out of control, a sense of dread ...

Radclyffe feared and despised her mother. In her own words:

> Always my mother. Violent and brainless. A fool but a terribly crafty and cruel fool for whom life had early become a distorting mirror in which she saw only her own reflection.

In two autobiographies, which were never published, Radclyffe described her mother as grasping, violent and capricious and wrote: 'I pity those whose memories of home have been rendered intolerable as have mine. They and I have lost a great sweetness in life.' Her mother had tried to abort her and described her as being like her father with her hands, nose, temper and perversity coming from him whom her mother described as 'the devil incarnate'.

Of her birth, Radclyffe wrote:

> A night of physical passion and then me, born solely of bodily desire, of animal impulse and nothing more. For I cannot believe those parents of mine could ever have known the love of the spirit. Nor did I bring peace into that distracted home by drawing their warring nature together. Quite the contrary. At the time of my birth a deadly quarrel was raging.

Indeed, her parents parted just a month after her birth. As we have seen, her father was an unreliable character. His father, Charles Radclyffe Hall, became president of the British Medical Association and founded a charitable sanatorium in Torquay. He was financially successful and married Esther Westhead who was also rich in her own right.

Although Radclyffe's father studied law at Oxford University he did not qualify and, thanks to a large allowance, had no need to work. Instead he hunted, kept horses and dogs and chased women, not all of whom were of his class. He met Radclyffe's mother, Mary Jane Sager, in 1878 and they were married within months as they wanted to legitimise the birth of their first daughter. Mary Jane's mother, who lived in Philadelphia in the USA, did not come to the wedding. After the wedding reception, 'Rat' said: 'You've heard of the glorious stars and stripes. Well, I've married one of the stars, may I never deserve the stripes.'

The marriage was a disaster from the first day and when

Radclyffe was born the doctor was not available, the nurse was at the chemist and 'Rat' was in bed with the maid. Radclyffe wrote later: 'When I was born my father was being blatantly and crudely unfaithful. The details were too base to record.'

Nor was the marriage break-up on friendly terms. On the contrary, Mary Jane claimed 'Rat' used violent and abusive language, beat her and deserted her when her elder daughter was dying and second daughter, Radclyffe, just born. 'Rat' denied the charges but, nevertheless, she was granted judicial separation, custody of her daughter and substantial maintenance.

But Mary Jane was left in a desperate state. She had an unwanted daughter and no house of her own. She did not want to return to Philadelphia and English society thought she was a vulgar, gold-digging American. At least she had her daughter christened in a Protestant church and Radclyffe would say later:

> My mother had me christened Marguerite. She could not have chosen a more inappropriate name. I detested it.

Mary Jane and Marguerite Radclyffe moved to a house in Notting Hill in west London with a nurse named Knott. The owner of the house and Knott would chat about their dislike of Marguerite's mother and when Marguerite asked why, she was sent to bed. Her mother was often absent, but when around her behaviour was erratic, with lots of laughter and tears. She treated the servants abominably.

Luckily for Marguerite her maternal grandmother, Diehl, came to stay, and behaved normally so that Marguerite would say later: 'Without her I think I must have died of sheer starvation of heart and spirit.' Grandma called her Tuggie and Marguerite said that through her she discovered

an altogether new sensation ... a sensation that made you discontented unless you were with the person you wanted to be near. A sensation that made you want to look at them and admire them and be praised by them and kissed by them. It was no less a factor than love.

The only problem was that Grandma kept returning to the USA. This is what Diana Souhami wrote about Marguerite's upbringing in her book *The Trials of Radclyffe Hall*:

There were few visitors to her mother's house. Social graces were not demanded of Marguerite nor learned by her ... She had lessons with her nurse in the mornings and a walk in Kensington Gardens. She needed special tuition which she did not receive. She liked to hear stories read aloud, she learned rudimentary arithmetic and to sing and play the piano. But she could not read or write. She stayed confused as to which letter was which.

Without children to play with she invented Daisy, an imaginary friend. She protected Daisy from the stained-glass dragon and played with her in the park. Daisy admired all Marguerite did. Her advent alarmed Nurse Knott, who suggested to Mary Jane that her daughter needed friends.

Told to desist from this game, Marguerite had a temper tantrum and bit her nurse on the hand. Ushered to her mother's bedroom, where her mother was brushing her hair, she refused to say her imaginary friend, her alter ego, did not exist. More than a game, it was an exercise in consolation, an endeavour to repair a fractured world. Her father had called her Daisy, and a Marguerite is a genus of daisy. Her mother saw in her face and manner an image of the man she loathed. She pushed her to the bed and beat her with the silver hairbrush. When she had finished she consigned her to the nurse and slammed the bedroom door. 'It was a hard whipping given and received in temper, an unfortunate whipping.' It was one of many administered while her mother was out of control. Its predictable effect was to inspire her daughter with defiance, hatred and rage.

She retreated inwards, was solitary, watchful, strange. She did not know how to play with children, trust a parent or how to feel safe. In the inchoate world of childhood, responses were formed by her and reactions made. She took into her feelings all that happened, sought control of her world, made emotional equations, disturbed connections, that echoed on into the books she was to write and the adult life she chose. Dark forces informed her early years. Abandonment elided with insecurity, hatred of her mother with aggrandizement of herself. Unfairness called for justice and violence for revenge.

Homosexuality

In the twentieth century homosexuality became more acceptable than it had been previously, and in the UK many rights are now enshrined in law: to marriage and civil union, adoption and parenting, employment, military service and equal access to healthcare, as well as the introduction of anti-bullying legislation.

However, in the early twentieth century, women did not

have the same freedom to pursue same-sex relationships as men. On the other hand, in many societies nor did women suffer the same harsh punishment. Nevertheless, homosexual women had to accept the fact that they were not seen as normal and were likely to be treated as outcasts.

Literary works in the late nineteenth century tended to dwell on male rather than female homosexuality, since the latter was not thought by the medical profession to be a significant issue. Some even felt there was no such thing as female homosexuality.

However, Havelock Ellis in Britain and the German sexologist Richard von Krafft-Ebing thought that lesbianism did exist, and indeed categorised it as a kind of insanity. For Krafft-Ebing it was a neurological disease, though he and Ellis disagreed on whether such homosexuality was a condition that would last for the whole of a woman's life. Ellis believed that women who felt love for others of the same sex would change their feelings after marriage, having experienced what he called a 'practical life'.

After her unsettled, not to say erratic, upbringing, Radclyffe continued to lead an unconventional life. With the inheritance from her now-dead father she leased a house in Church Street, Kensington and moved in with her grandmother. She had an affair with the opera singer Agnes Nicholls, but this did not last long, though Radclyffe would take other lovers to see her singing at the opera in Covent Garden.

She now had money, freedom and a definite sexual orientation which she wanted to make clear. She used the name Peter, though this did not stick. She wore her hair in a style that made her look like a young man, and dressed accordingly. At the same time she rode horses, hunted foxes, kept dogs and budgerigars and started a stamp collection.

She wanted it to be clear that she had no interest in affairs with men. As the novelist Violet Hunt wrote: 'Man is vile to her and I believe that is why she will never marry.' Radclyffe fell in love with Violet and wrote this to her:

Perhaps even now you are thinking me impertinent as you read this letter. I can't help it Violet, I must risk that. If I can't always say the things I am feeling when we are together it is because you have built a brick wall around yourself and I must not venture to get inside it. No doubt you have many good reasons for wanting it to be there. I have never met anyone who could so repulse affection as you can in your own sweet way. If you are angry with me what can I say except that I am so fond of you? I will never bother you to read this sort of thing again.

She was not deterred by the fact that the women she fancied were married. For example, she pursued Jane Randolph, an American with a businessman husband and three children; when the husband died she brought Jane and the children from Washington DC to live with her and her grandmother in Kensington.

However, while still living with Jane, Marguerite began an affair with one of her cousins, Dolly Diehl, and, when Jane Randolph remarried, Dolly moved in to live with Marguerite in Kensington and the two of them travelled to France, Italy and Germany together. Meanwhile Marguerite continued to write her simple poetry:

Oh the awful pity of it all,
That I ever learned to care for you
That we ever chanced to meet at all

> Since we neither of us could be true.
> My love is a bird with a broken wing,
> Alone in a stormy night;
> My love is a lark that forgets to sing
> And dies with the morning light.

and received good reviews. The *Evening Standard* wrote of her 'sincerity and sweetness', the *Queen* of her 'vigorous, joyful youth, thankful for the right to exist in such a lovely world', and *The Lady* of the 'real feeling and the power to express it'.

Marguerite's next affair was with the tennis player Toupie Lowther. They booked into the Savoy hotel where Marguerite met one of Toupie's friends, Mabel Batten. Mabel had earlier enjoyed an affair with Edward, Prince of Wales – by this time King Edward VII was 50 and Mabel's husband, George, 74. She liked to use strange words to describe people. For example 'sporks' were very dull, 'poggers' were flirts, 'sneevish' meant irritable while 'poons' were good types and entertaining. When Marguerite met Mabel they both decided they were 'poons'.

Marguerite wrote later about Mabel in notes for an autobiography:

> I was as wax in her hands, but those hands were entirely trustworthy. She was to become a spur to my work and from the first my true unfailing inspiration. She was a whole generation older, but of so gay and youthful a spirit, of so balanced, generous and masterly a mind, courteous, kindly and gallant a heart …

Mabel had been born in Calcutta and had travelled, while growing up, to Japan, North Africa and Europe. She had studied music in Bruges and Dresden. She could sing and with a lively laugh, dark blue eyes, a big bust and small waist, was attractive to men. Her cousin, Una Troubridge (of whom more later), said of her: 'She accepted homage as a matter of course. She had always received it.'

When Radclyffe met Mabel in 1906 they immediately liked each other. Mabel liked Radclyffe's poetry and Radclyffe wrote of her:

I must work hard to be worthy of her friendship. What I am I owe to her. She criticised my work but so justly that I could not feel resentment. She took me and very gradually proceeded to rub off the sharp and ugly corners.

And Mabel approved of Marguerite's money, poems and jewels.

However, Marguerite was still living with Dolly Diehl and it was only gradually over the next two years that she began her affair with Mabel who, up to that point, had not had a lesbian relationship. When Mabel visited the Kensington house and saw a portrait of Marguerite's great-great-grandfather, the surgeon John Hall, she realised how like him Marguerite looked and from that moment Mabel called Marguerite John.

As Diana Souhami wrote:

More than a fond nickname, this was a symbolic rechristening. It released Marguerite from the hated name her mother had given her and from her discomfort at being a woman. It fed her fantasy and turned her mother's curse into a boast. 'You are Radclyffe through and through, not an ounce of your blood is mine.' By reconstruction she was not the same gender. She was an English squire from a time-honoured family, with horses, hounds and a wife. For Mabel too it defined the partnership in society's terms.

Mabel became 'Ladye' so from that time onwards they became John and Ladye.

Mabel's husband, George, was effectively abandoned and Dolly Diehl moved on so that John and Ladye lived near each other in Chelsea, went on many holidays together and became very happy, especially after grandmother Diehl and husband George both died in 1910.

However, in true Marguerite (John) style she became bored. Her head was turned by Phoebe Hoare, who was married to Oliver Hoare of the Hoare banking family. They had an affair – much to Ladye's irritation – but when the war broke out in August 1914 this affair ended. John and Ladye's life together was then damaged again, this time by a car accident which nearly killed Ladye, leaving her in a wheelchair.

The outbreak of the First World War in August 1914 did not improve matters. To save money John and Ladye left 59 Cadogan Square, leased it and moved to John's house in Malvern, Worcestershire. And as we have seen, her affair with Phoebe Hoare ended.

John turned to writing, although her style was clumsy at first; Ladye edited her stories and John sent them to literary magazines. Most of them were rejected and John said: 'They always came back in my own stamped envelope – I grew to dread my own handwriting.'

As it happened Ladye knew the publisher William Heinemann, and contacted him. John and Ladye had lunch with him in June 1915 and John was staggered by his praise, saying: 'He seemed quite willing to do all the talking and I heard such words of praise that I could scarcely believe my ears.' He advised John to write a full-length novel for him, but she had not completed it when he died in 1920 and it took John another five years to get it into print.

The next big event in John's life occurred on 1 August 1915 when she met Ladye's cousin Una Troubridge, who thought John, with her beautiful eyes and raffish smile, was very good-looking. She said later: 'It was not the countenance of a young woman but of a very handsome young man.'

Una Troubridge

Lady Una Vincenzo Troubridge was born Margot Elena Gertrude Taylor on 8 March 1887. Her family nicknamed her Una and she herself chose her middle name, Vincenzo, after her Florentine relatives. Raised in Montpelier Square, London, she became a student at the Royal College of Art. After her father died in 1907, leaving her with very little money, marriage seemed the sensible option and she married Captain Ernest Troubridge in October 1908.

It was not a successful marriage. Ernest had been married before, to a Canadian, Edith Duffus, in 1891. She died nine years later when her fourth child was stillborn. Ernest was 46 compared with Una's twenty by the time they married in 1908, and he had acquired syphilis. Soon after their wedding and honeymoon in Paris, he sailed to Malta and stayed there for two years. However, he had already passed on his syphilis to Una who would write later:

He had no right to marry. Especially to marry a healthy girl young enough to be his daughter. And I would have escaped 14 years of invalidism and its after effects.

Diana Souhami would write:

> For years she monitored her treatments for this infection: daily visits to doctors, referrals to gynaecologists, injections, vaccines and analyses of smears. It made her disgusted with him and herself, hypochondriacal about every symptom of ill-health, rejecting of her daughter ... whom she considered tainted like herself, and disdainful of everything to do with sex. 'The physical never mattered to me anyway after the first misery' ...

They had a daughter named Andrea but, by the time Ernest Troubridge had served successfully enough in the Royal Navy during the First World War to be promoted to admiral and knighted in 1919, they were separated.

As we have seen, Una had met Radclyffe (now known as John) in 1915 as Mabel Batten (Ladye), Radclyffe's lover at the time, was Una's cousin. When Ladye died in 1916, Una and John pursued their relationship and began living together in 1917. By the early 1920s they had moved to 10 Stirling Street, London which was close to where Una had been brought up. By this time their relationship was so intense that Una wrote in her diary: 'I could not, having come to know her, imagine life without her.' John was not as full of love for Una as Una was for her and said: 'How do I know I shall care for you in six months' time?'

Una wanted John to care for her forever. She rented an artist's studio in Tite Street, Chelsea and made John her main subject. Drawing her and making a sculpture of her meant they were together all day.

However, John had not fully let go of her devotion to Ladye. When Ladye died in 1916, Una wrote of John's reaction:

John's grief was overwhelming and was intensified by remorse. She blamed herself bitterly and uncompromisingly that she had allowed her affection for me to trespass upon her exclusive devotion to Ladye, that she had brought me so closely into their home life, thereby as she thought, marring the happiness of Ladye's last months on earth ... she saw no excuse for herself in the fact, fully realized by Ladye, of the twenty-four years' difference in their ages and her comparative youth. She even reproached herself for that last day at Maidenhead. She turned to me instinctively in her despair as she was always, thank God, to turn to me in all trouble throughout her life, and yet, paradoxically, her desire for expiation was such that I think there was a time when, had she only considered herself, she would have put me out of her life and offered me up as a sacrifice to loyalty. But even in the depths she was incapable at all times of considering herself alone, and there is proof of that in an incident during Ladye's last illness. Day and night John had sat beside her, awaiting what she knew to be the inevitable end but clinging to the hope that before it came there might be a momentary return to full consciousness that would allow her to speak of her deathless devotion and to receive absolution for any real or imagined shortcomings. But when, before the end, the doctor told her that consciousness could be induced by an injection, if it was for any reason desirable, she utterly refused to accept consolation for herself at the risk of rousing Ladye to possible pain ... and she let her go in silence.

The Well of Loneliness

The Well of Loneliness, Radclyffe Hall's most famous novel, was originally called *Stephen* and was published in 1928.

The novel's plot revolves around Stephen Gordon, a woman who lives within the homosexual milieu of Paris and who identifies as an 'invert'. 'Invert' was the contemporary psychological term for homosexual, and Stephen Gordon recognises the trait within herself after reading Krafft-Ebing's *Psychopathia Sexualis.*

Havelock Ellis wrote a foreword for *The Well of Loneliness*, and the novel was essentially a plea for tolerance for inverts, on the grounds that they suffered from what was really an accident of birth. Hall agreed with Ellis and Krafft-Ebing rather than with Freud, who held that same-sex attraction was caused by childhood difficulties and upsets and therefore could be cured.

Press coverage was not shy about suggesting that the novel contained elements of 'sexual relations between Lesbian women', and photographs of Radclyffe Hall in her habitual 'mannish' attire usually accompanied the articles. Her monocle, cropped hair and masculine suits were clear signals for newspaper readers of the time.

Although Radclyffe Hall is most famous for *The Well of Loneliness*, she had also brought a slander action in 1918 when she challenged St George Lane Fox-Pitt for calling her 'a grossly immoral woman' following a reading of her research paper at the Society for Psychical Research. Radclyffe's lawyer said that it was 'as horrible an accusation as could be made and could only mean that the plaintiff was an unchaste and immoral woman who was addicted to unnatural vice'. As it happened, the jury found for Radclyffe and awarded her £500 (£30,000 in today's money) in damages.

When *The Well of Loneliness* was published Radclyffe was already a very successful novelist. Indeed, her novel *Adam's Breed*, which was about the spiritual awakening of an Italian head waiter, had become a bestseller and would win the Prix Femina and James Tait Black Prize. Although she had long considered writing a novel about sexual inversion, Radclyffe now felt such a novel would stand a good chance of a considerable readership. Nevertheless, she realised the risk she would be taking and obtained permission to proceed from her partner, Una Troubridge.

Radclyffe's ambitions in writing and publishing *The Well of Loneliness* were to help put an end to public silence about homosexuality and bring about 'a more tolerant understanding' and also to 'spur all classes of inverts to make good through hard work and sober and useful living'. As we shall see, she told a publisher she would not allow any alterations, saying:

> I have put my pen at the service of some of the most persecuted and misunderstood people in the world. So far as I know nothing of the kind has ever been attempted before in fiction.

In the novel, the central figure, Stephen Gordon, is born to upper-class parents who had expected to have a boy – they therefore give her the name Stephen, regardless. She grows up wanting to be a boy in every way, keeping her hair short and hating to wear dresses. At the age of seven, she develops a crush on the housemaid.

Her affectionate father tries to understand her through

contemporary writings on sex and psychology, though her mother remains distant and disdainful. Eventually her father dies without having revealed to either his wife or his daughter that he has discovered that Stephen is an invert.

At 21 Stephen falls in love with Angela Crossby, the wife of a neighbour, though it is clear that Angela is using Stephen to stave off boredom more than anything else. Finally the truth about Stephen's feelings for Angela becomes known to Stephen's mother, who derides her for 'presuming to use the word love in connection with … these unnatural cravings of your unbalanced mind and undisciplined body', to which Stephen responds that her love for Angela is as real as that of any heterosexual lover. Stephen then discovers her late father's research, including a book by Krafft-Ebing, revealing to her the truth of her sexual identity as an invert.

Through various adventures as a novelist in Paris and an ambulance-driver in the First World War, Stephen ends up in a relationship with a comrade from the war, Mary Llewellyn. However, that does not work out, and in the end, to ensure Mary's future happiness, Stephen uses subterfuge to get Mary to take up with a male friend of Stephen's from her teenage years. Stephen's final plea is: 'Give us also the right to our existence!'

Before exploring the controversy the book provoked, it is worth noting that the only sexual reference it contained was the words: 'And that night they were not divided.'

Publication, planned for October 1928, was brought forward to July when it was discovered that another book on lesbianism, Compton Mackenzie's *Extraordinary Women*, was scheduled for publication in September.

The first publishing house to be approached was Cassell, where Newman Flower had high hopes for the book after the success of *Adam's Breed*. However, Radclyffe wrote him a letter which included that she 'could not consent to one word being changed' and that he was to 'stand behind this book to the last ditch and go all out on it for the sakes of those for whom I have written'. She concluded:

> Having attained literary success I have put my pen at the service of some of the most persecuted and misunderstood people in the world. In a word I have written a long and very serious novel entirely upon the subject of sexual inversion. So far as I know nothing of the kind has ever been attempted before in fiction.

Within days Newman Fowler replied that he thought it was a fine book but not one he could publish as it would harm the rest of his list.

Charles Evans at William Heinemann also turned it down, saying that he felt it was propaganda and 'inevitably the publishers of it will have to meet not only severe criticism but a chorus of fanatical abuse which, although unjustifiable, may nevertheless do them considerable damage. That consequence we are not prepared to face.'

However, when Radclyffe's agent Audrey Heath sent the book to Jonathan Cape, he could see its commercial potential. Cape published *The Well of Loneliness* with a black cover and a plain jacket and sent review copies only to the newspapers and magazines he thought would review it without trying to wind up controversy. In fact, early reviews were mixed. Some critics felt it was too preachy while others found the writing sloppy. Others were full of praise. *Cassell's Weekly* wrote:

One cannot say what effect this book will have on the public attitude of silence or derision, but every reader will agree with Mr Havelock Ellis in the preface that 'the poignant situations are set forth with a complete absence of offence'.

Jonathan Cape offered Radclyffe an advance of £500 (£30,000 in today's money) and proposed a print run of 1,250 copies. Radclyffe was concerned about her potential financial liability and it was agreed that she and Cape would share any legal costs which, as we shall see, would prove to be a fortunate provision.

On publication in the UK large advertisements were placed in the *Yorkshire Post*, the *Spectator*, the *Sunday Times*, the *Observer*, the *Times Literary Supplement* and for whatever day was finally chosen for publication, in seven daily papers.

Cape were becoming more bullish and the print run was increased to 5,200 copies with paper ordered for a further 5,000, and the selling price was put at 15 shillings (75p or £45.00 in today's money). The editor of the *Observer*, James Garvin, happened to be married to Una Troubridge's sister and Radclyffe wrote to him:

When I tell you that I wrote this book from a sense of duty, a sense of duty which I dared not disobey ... I have tried to bring the thing out into God's air and light – for the Truth must never be feared, since it is the truth. It would be childish for me to pretend that I do not know how much your support in the *Observer* would contribute from the first appearance of my book on July 24th towards its success – above all to its reception in the proper spirit, the spirit of desire for impartial justice and understanding towards an unhappy and very important section of the community.

In spite of this plea, Garvin did not support the book and the *Observer* was one of the few national papers not to review it. His wife disliked Una's relationship with Radclyffe and the subject of lesbianism.

In the event, as Radclyffe and Una discovered on touring bookshops, *The Well of Loneliness* was everywhere. There were rows in the windows of WH Smith as well as *The Times* bookshop, Trueloves and Harrods.

Not all publicity for *The Well of Loneliness* was unfavourable. Indeed, there was a glowing review in the *Sunday Times*, and in the *Saturday Review* L.P. Hartley praised the book's force and sincerity, its powerful appeal and its passages of great beauty. *TP's Weekly* noted that 'poignant situations are set forth with a complete absence of offence'. In the *Evening Standard*, Arnold Bennett described the book's 'notable psychological and sociological significance' and said it was 'honest, convincing and extremely courageous.' On 17 August 1928 the *Daily Telegraph* wrote that *The Well of Loneliness* was 'truly remarkable, a work of art finely conceived and finely written'.

However not all the reviews were so kind. Leonard Woolf in the *Nation* said the book was a failure and Cyril Connolly in the *New Statesman* wrote that it was 'long, tedious, absolutely humourless and a melodramatic description of a subject which has nothing melodramatic about it'. He summed up the views of many in Great Britain at that time:

> *The Well of Loneliness* may be a brave book to have written, but let us hope it will pave the way for someone to write a better. Homosexuality is, after all, as rich in comedy as in tragedy, and it is time it was emancipated from the aura of distinguished damnation and religious martyrdom which surrounds its so fiercely aggressive apologists.

Out in the bookshop market, by 2 August 1928, Harrods and *The Times* bookshop had sold all their copies and reordered twice. Jonathan Cape were planning a third print run.

However, it soon became clear that it would not all be plain sailing. Being aware of the prejudices of James Douglas, editor of the *Sunday Express*, Cape did not send him a copy of *The Well of Loneliness*. Nevertheless, he acquired a copy. After reading it, he wrote an article published on 19 August 1928 under the heading 'A Book That Must Be Suppressed', in which he said that 'we must face the task of cleaning ourselves from the leprosy of these lepers, and making the air clean and wholesome once more':

It is no use to say that the novel possesses 'fine qualities' or that its author is an 'accomplished' artist. It is no defence to say that the author is sincere or that she is frank, or that there is delicacy in her art.

The answer is that the adroitness and cleverness of the book intensifies its moral danger. It is a seductive and insidious piece of special pleading designed to display perverted decadence as a martyrdom inflicted upon these outcasts by a cruel society. It flings a veil of sentiment over their depravity. It even suggests that their self-made debasement is unavoidable because they cannot save themselves.

This terrible doctrine may commend itself to certain schools of pseudo-scientific thought, but it cannot be reconciled with the Christian religion or with the Christian doctrine of freewill. Therefore, it must be fought to the bitter end by the Christian Churches. This is the radical difference between paganism and Christianity.

If Christianity does not destroy this doctrine, then this doctrine will destroy it, together with the civilisation it has built on the ruins of paganism. These moral derelicts are not cursed from their birth. Their downfall is caused by their own act and their own will. They are damned because they choose to be damned, not because they are doomed from the beginning.

We must protect our children against their specious fallacies and sophistries. Therefore, we must banish their propaganda from our bookshops and libraries. I would rather give a healthy boy or a healthy girl a phial of prussic acid than this novel. Poison kills the body, but moral poison kills the soul.

What, then, is to be done? The book must at once be withdrawn. I hope the author and the publishers will realise that they have made a grave mistake, and will without delay do all in their power to repair it. If they hesitate to do so, the book must be suppressed by the process of law … I appeal to the Home Secretary to set the law in motion. He should instruct the Director of Public Prosecutions to consider whether *The Well of Loneliness* is fit for circulation, and, if not, to take action to prevent its being further circulated.

Finally, let me warn our novelists and our men of letters that literature as well as morality is in peril. Fiction of this type is an injury to good literature. It makes the profession of literature fall into disrepute. Literature has not yet recovered from the harm done to it by the Oscar Wilde scandal. It should keep its house in order.

Following the attacks in the *Sunday Express*, a copy of the book was sent to the home secretary, Sir William Joynson-Hicks, by Jonathan Cape, with the following note:

If it is shown to us that the best interests of the public will be served by withdrawing the book from circulation we will be ready to do this and to accept the full consequences as publishers. We are not however prepared to withdraw it at the behest of the Editor of the *Sunday Express.*

However, the *Express* won in the end because Joynson-Hicks, after consultation with colleagues and the Lord Chancellor, concluded that the book was indeed 'both obscene and indecent'. It dealt with and supported a depraved practice. He wrote to Cape that the book was 'gravely detrimental to the public interest. I am advised, moreover, that the book can be suppressed by criminal proceedings. I prefer, however, to believe that in view of your letter you will accept my decision and withdraw the book, and this I now ask you to do.'

Cape were prepared to do this and told the printer to wait. However, Radclyffe Hall was outraged and wrote to the *Daily Herald* which printed her letter on 24 August:

If seriously written psychological novels are to be subjected to arbitrary attack from the Home Office, which attacks result in their being withdrawn, what chance has our sane and well educated public of obtaining the best output from publisher and author?

Must there never be any new pastures for the writer? Never any new aspects of social problems presented to the adult and open minded reader? Is the reader to be treated like a kind of mental dyspeptic whose literary food must be predigested by Government Office before consumption?

Such action can only insult the public intelligence and discourage our authors from writing sincerely, especially our younger and less established authors some of whom may yet have new messages for us. On behalf of English literature I must protest against such unwarrantable interference.

The court case

The prosecution began on Friday 9 November 1928. Radclyffe had drawn up a list of over 160 people whom she felt would appear in court to speak on her behalf. Whether they would or not, the majority of them pleaded other appointments they had that day. Nevertheless, the court was packed and there were 40 ready to help. Radclyffe described them as 'eminent men and women of good will'.

It was up to the court to decide whether *The Well of Loneliness* was an obscene publication according to the law of the land. The relevant legislation was the Obscene Publications Act of 1857, which prohibited the sale of books, pictures and 'other articles' that 'depraved and corrupted' the morals of young people and shocked 'the common feelings of decency in any well-regulated mind'. Under this act, D.H. Lawrence's novel *The Rainbow* of 1915 had been tried, condemned and ordered to be burned in the same court – also after one of James Douglas's outbursts.

In fact, there was no law which criminalised sex between women. Indeed, an attempt to pass such legislation in 1921 had been defeated.

The magistrate did not allow the defence witnesses to testify and, in the afternoon, he dismissed everyone saying that in a week's time the court would reconvene and he would give his verdict. On that day he said, after maintaining that *The Well of Loneliness* dealt solely with 'unnatural offences':

> There is not a single word from beginning to end of this book which suggests that anyone with these horrible tendencies is in the least blameworthy or that they should in any way

resist them. The characters in this book who indulge in these horrible vices are presented to us as attractive people and put forward for our admiration; and those who object to these vices are sneered at in the book as prejudiced, foolish and cruel.

Not merely that, but there is a much more serious matter, the actual physical acts of these women indulging in unnatural vices are described in the most alluring terms; their result is described as giving these women extraordinary rest, contentment and pleasure; and not merely that, but it is actually put forward that it improves their mental balance and capacity.

However, all this criticism was not entirely bad news. The storm brought publicity which meant more sales. In the USA, the publisher, Pascal Covici, gave Radclyffe a staggering advance of $10,000 which was about £2,500 or £150,000 in today's money.

He then sold the book at $5 rather than a more normal $2. The book was also selling strongly in Europe and the publicity, not all unfavourable, continued. *In Time and Tide*, Hugh Walpole wrote:

James Douglas, Joynson-Hicks and Charles Biron have caused certain subjects to be discussed, inquired into and pleasingly investigated as never before in the history of this hypocritical country.

Following legal action in Britain, *The Well of Loneliness* was also tried legally in the USA. Again the whole story became national news and one journal described Radclyffe Hall thus:

She is Byronese in appearance and her friends all call her John. Her jewels, large emeralds sunk in platinum, are the only softening note in her mannish profile. Her short blonde hair is combed straight back and her blue suit is Bond Street tailored. Her shirt is blue linen with a standing collar and the tie navy. She wears a monocle on a cord, a watch in her handkerchief pocket suspended on a leather fob from the lapel buttonhole. In the evening Miss Hall wears a moiré tuxedo with a black satin stock and a ruffled shirt front. Her hat is a large Montmartre.

The court adjourned, the judges went away for eleven days with copies of *The Well of Loneliness* and Ernst's brief. They reconvened on 19 April 1929 and gave their verdict:

The book in question deals with a delicate social problem which in itself cannot be said to be in violation of the law unless it is written in such a manner as to make it obscene. This is a criminal prosecution and as judges of the facts and the law we are not called upon nor is it within our province to recommend or advise against the reading of any book, nor is it within our province to pass an opinion as to the merits or demerits thereof, but only as to whether the same is in violation of the law. The people must establish that the defendants are guilty of violation of Section 1141 beyond a reasonable doubt, After a careful reading of the entire book, we conclude that the book in question is not in violation of the law.

Sales rocketed and Radclyffe received a royalty cheque for $64,000 (£4,000, or nearly £1 million in today's money). Nevertheless, Radclyffe was not happy because her home country had rejected her and she was not sure where to live.

She chose Rye in Sussex and moved there with Una where they were received as a respected married couple. Radclyffe wrote a new novel, *The Master of the House*, and it was launched by Foyle's at a literary lunch with 700 guests in March 1932.

Unfortunately, the book was the subject of poor reviews in the *Telegraph*, *The Times*, the *Times Literary Supplement* and the *Spectator* – the latter accused Radclyffe of sentimentality, while the *Saturday Review of Literature* called the book 'a bad novel for her to hide in' after *The Well of Loneliness*. The book did not sell well, either in Britain or the USA.

Radclyffe Hall's final years

Radclyffe spent the 1930s living and travelling with Una Troubridge but it was not altogether a happy time for either of them, largely because Radclyffe could not give up her habit of being attracted to other women. She had a long affair with a Russian girl, Eugenia Souline, which, needless to say, Una found extremely irritating.

When Radclyffe died in a furnished flat in Dolphin Square, in 1943, Una wrote:

> Immediately after her death I was besieged by the press with inquiries as to whether she had left any completed book or any work sufficiently advanced for publication.
>
> On the impulse of the moment and much too unhappy to use my judgment I told the simple truth: that I had given her my promise that I would destroy the book upon which she had been engaged. Not unnaturally this statement led to a spate of press comment and it also procured me some tedious

letters in which I was warned by a number of self-constituted advisers that I should be gravely wronging Radclyffe Hall's public if I took upon myself this act of vandalism. I answered a few of them and pointed out that such a decision had rested exclusively with the writer herself and that I had no alternative to that of honourably carrying out her wishes.

But there was one correspondent who had to receive a more detailed answer. This was an unknown member of the public who wrote assuming that the book was to be destroyed because Radclyffe Hall, having returned to the subject of sexual inversion, had in the end lacked the courage to permit publication. My reply made it abundantly clear that John had never been in any doubt that *The Well of Loneliness* contained all that she had to say on that subject; that she had never for a moment contemplated a sequel or any return to that aspect of nature, but that had she done so she would very certainly have published all that she had to say.

The true reason for the destruction of the book was a simple one: she had, during the closing years of her life, been very deeply hurt by someone and when she knew that her days were numbered she had forgiven both the injury and the person concerned. But she felt that into the writing of that book she had almost unconsciously allowed the intrusion of a measure of her personal suffering and natural resentment and, as she said when she told me to destroy it: 'It isn't forgiveness if one leaves a record that might be recognized and give pain.'

CHAPTER 4

JOHN LOGIE BAIRD –
'SEEING BY WIRELESS'

John Logie Baird is famous for his reputed invention of the television.

In reality it was more complicated than that, but he did indeed demonstrate the first working television system on 26 January 1926. He was also the inventor of the first publicly demonstrated colour television system.

Baird was born in August 1888 in Helensburgh in Dunbartonshire, Scotland, the youngest of four children of the Reverend John Baird, a minister of the Church of Scotland. He went to Larchfield Academy, now part of Lomond School, in Helensburgh, then on to the Glasgow and West of Scotland Technical College and finally to the University of Glasgow. While he was at the college he took a series of engineering apprentice jobs.

While he was at university the First World War broke out, but he was deemed unfit to serve and instead worked for the Clyde Valley Electrical Power Company which was engaged in munitions manufacture.

He found himself working in unpleasant conditions and, never the most healthy of men, he suffered from chills, colds and influenza and was often absent from work. As a result he stood no chance of promotion and eventually resigned.

He said later:

If I had remained travelling along the straight road of an engineering career, I should either be dead by now or a hopeless, broken-spirited object. To break my career seemed to those about me the act of an irresponsible madman, the throwing away of all my expensive training. If the choice was between slavery and madness, I preferred madness – there seemed no middle course. 'Are there no ways but these alone, madman or slave must man be one!' It seemed so in my case. If I remained an engineer I saw nothing before me but a vista of grey days, of unrelieved drudgery. Coughing and shivering through the winters, what hope to force my way through the mob of lusty competitors?

Baird then went into business on his own and was successful with his invention and development of a product which he conceived because he suffered, among his other infirmities, from cold feet.

This ailment was invariably caused by damp, and Baird mused that while civilisation had come up with the watertight boot, it had neglected another fundamental, the watertight sock, so he set about remedying this oversight. He heated wet socks to burning point, but found them damp again within a very short time. Wads of paper between the foot and the sock did the trick, however, and the relief was great. A bewildered landlady found him with sheets of toilet paper wrapped round his feet, but clearly the project had to be advanced beyond this rudimentary and impractical stage. He commented afterwards:

Papers under socks were not feasible, so I broached the sock maker and, after many peregrinations, discovered two things. Firstly, the Trade does not recognise such things as socks. Socks are 'gent's half-hose'. Secondly the home of 'gent's half-hose' is Hinckley. From Hinckley I got six dozen specially made unbleached half-hose. Then I sprinkled them with borax and put them in large envelopes printed with 'The Baird Undersock' and containing a pamphlet describing their advantages and containing testimonials.

Baird's product was worn beneath the ordinary sock and was damp-proof. He rented a one-room office at 196 St Vincent Street, in Glasgow's busy city centre, where he masterminded the project, even adding a few home-made testimonials to speed the 'undersock' on its way. He turned a back-street attic above a hotel into a tiny factory, churning out the socks himself by night and going round the shops with them, when he could find time, the following day. An advertisement for sales representatives in the Glasgow *Herald* brought dozens of replies, and soon he had men travelling all over Scotland and as far south as London, where Selfridge's bought six dozen pairs. His old cronies found socks arriving through the post in the hope that they might push them among friends. Archibald Thom got a pair, and so did the future Brigadier Prain, now at the Western Front. Baird made advertising history when he sent a squad of women round the city streets with sandwich boards. Newspapers used pictures with the caption: 'First Sandwich Women in Glasgow.' He followed this with another eye-catching stunt, a life-size wooden model of the new armoured tank being used by the British army, standing almost nine feet high and almost twice as long, with realistic side guns, which trundled through the streets propelled from inside by two hard-working men. The tank bore the proud legend: 'The Baird Undersock Keeps the Soldier's Feet in Perfect Health.'

The undersocks were sold in chemists' shops, but the biggest sales were in drapery stores. When the Royal Polytechnic, the Selfridge's of Glasgow, bought a dozen pairs, Baird was perplexed to find they were not on display. He swiftly rallied his friends, handed them money, and had them wend their way to the store, where the astonished sales staff found themselves facing unprecedented demand. The result was immediate and gratifying. A buyer was rushed to Baird's premises at St Vincent Street where three times he found the office closed. A note was left and Baird obligingly turned up at the store and sold 600 pairs on the spot. The Polytechnic had a special table set up in an entrance and a front window bedecked with the Baird undersock.

He said later:

> The result, of course, was an immediate rush by the inquisitive public. Not only so, but Copeland and Lye and the other big stores wanted to be in on this new line, which was booming at the Polytechnic! My whole stock was sold at once and I booked further substantial orders.

His sock business was so successful that in September 1918 he formed the Baird Undersock Company. It made £200 (£12,000 in today's money) a week, of which Baird was able to bank £195.

However, yet again, Baird's health let him down. A very bad cold with bronchial complications put him in a nursing home where, in great frustration, he watched his business suffer and was eventually forced to close it down. Nevertheless, he had made a profit of £1,600 (£96,000 in today's money); he realised that he had made more money in eighteen months than he would have earned in twelve years at Clyde Valley Electrical Power. He took the opportunity to escape Scotland, where the climate was gradually killing him, and sailed to Trinidad in the West Indies.

What has all this to do with Baird's eventual invention of the television?

In fact, it seems that alongside all this he had been quietly engaged in early experiments that would lead to the momentous discovery. As Tom McArthur and Peter Waddell wrote in *The Secret Life of John Logie Baird*:

> Baird's departure for the Caribbean affords an opportunity to appraise not only his own progress towards the realization of his goal, but also the steps which other pioneers had taken along the same road. Many of his contemporaries believed, wrongly, that after he had struggled for so many years in order to become a skilled electrical engineer he threw it all away in the pursuit of quick profits. To them his work on television in Hastings a few years later seemed to be merely the latest and most promising of a string of schemes designed to make a fortune.
>
> It will be seen, when the competition he encountered is examined, that it suited Baird to allow this view to persist. He found it politic to pretend that his work on television had very little substance prior to his experiments in Hastings. In fact the reverse was true, as will be demonstrated by details which have now come to light. Of course, he hoped that television might one day make him rich but, when he had to make the choice, he showed his true colours and threw out the chance of becoming a millionaire. He left others to cash in on his early work while, untrammelled by their demands to stand still and consolidate, he wandered into new lines of research. It now appears that from the start Baird basically sought money for the prime reason of gaining freedom to persevere with electrical vision. College had taught him the fundamentals of his calling, but his dream subject was not on the syllabus. There was little that anyone could teach him in this field, and so he researched alone. His hotchpotch of commercial ventures were merely stepping-stones to television.

Baird himself wrote in an article in the *Daily Express* in January 1926:

> I began my experiments in 1912 and met with great difficulties – lack of capital, shortness of time caused by the need to earn a living, and the knowledge that all over the globe, some of the best brains of the scientific world, backed by the possession of splendidly-equipped laboratories and limitless capital, were trying to complete the discovery in front of me. However, I saved my earnings and worked far into the night, sometimes having to stop experimenting because of the strain.

The same article makes another telling point. One of Baird's leading business partners in television was Belfast-born Captain Oliver George Hutchinson, whom Baird elsewhere describes as having met for the first time in London in 1922. Yet the *Express* article states:

> Then Captain Hutchinson, whom I had met at the Argyll works in 1912, came to my assistance and found capital when I was in financial straits.

Close associates confirm that they gleaned the impression that both Baird and Hutchinson had been apprentices in the same workshop, adding credence to the *Express* story. This sort of anomaly makes one wary of accepting at face value those accounts of early television which Baird intended for public consumption. The scenes described are probably accurate enough, but the dates, places and even the people were changed on occasions to protect the inventor's interests. He compiled his autobiographical notes in the summer of 1941, but portions were rewritten from articles already published in newspapers and magazines years before, versions to which he was therefore committed. The birth of television had already become something of a legend and had passed into the history books. It would have been difficult, and at that time, with the Second World War raging, pointlessly controversial to do an about-turn and change those oft-quoted facts and dates.

One of Baird's earliest biographers, R. Tiltman, writing in 1933, managed to draw Baird on some of his early attempts. He described how Baird carried out a great deal of experimental work involving electricity and the construction of selenium cells while attending college and university. This was not undertaken in the academic laboratories; the regular curriculum precluded original experiments. He depicts Baird, instead, operating in the makeshift lab of his boyhood, the kitchen of the house in Helensburgh. There he apparently tried to devise a system of talking pictures and made sunlight ring a bell. The German science journalist Egon Larsen, who knew Baird for many years up to 1946, the year of Baird's death, also recounts some of Baird's early work in television.

Sir J.D. Percy, later a director of Baird Television Ltd., wrote an article for *Motor News* of 26 June 1926 in which he quoted Baird as saying that he had been carrying out experiments more than ten years before (i.e. in 1915). Percy's article supports this by relating an account of the inventor in Yoker, Glasgow, in 1915.

Of his continued work on television while he was in Trinidad Baird himself wrote in a newspaper article in 1936:

Then my health broke down and I decided to go to Trinidad.

There I would not only recover my health, thus enabling me to carry on with television, I would also make some money, which I could spend on experiments … The only progress I made in that West Indies year was towards television. I spent my nights in the jungle working out problems, and on my return to England I was ready for new experiments.

When he returned to England his work on television increased. However, he could not fail to notice news in scientific magazines of others making progress in the same field, often with better facilities and more financial backing. Baird was in contact with some of them and, in some cases, accepted their help.

While others had relatively sophisticated equipment Baird had to resort to string and sealing wax, biscuit tins and darning needles and an assortment of basic materials.

To make ends meet he rented a tiny shop in Lupus Street in London and tried to market West Indian produce. However, it soon became clear that few people were interested in his unbranded mango chutney and guava jelly. He moved into very modest premises in Bloomsbury and started to answer advertisements in *The Times* headed 'Business Opportunities'. This brought him into contact with a number of dubious characters keen to extract what was left of his capital.

Nevertheless, he did start to make money again when he heard of consignments of Australian honey at the docks. He bought two tons and advertised in *The Times* and the *Morning Post*. He was successful in receiving orders. His business activities kept being interrupted by bouts of ill health, but in 1923 Baird moved to Hastings in Sussex and his work on television continued.

As McArthur and Waddle wrote:

One evening just before dusk, early in 1923, a curious procession wound its way up West Hill in the Sussex resort of Hastings. Above the shore, four boy scouts laboriously hauled a trek cart accompanied and aided by a mop-haired man in an overlong coat. The trek cart's contents were bulky and covered, and the man tended and steadied them as though they were precious. On reaching the summit he unloaded his mysterious burden and dismissed the boys with their cart. One was allowed to remain, and what he witnessed gives a rare glimpse of John Logie Baird conducting one of his previously unsuspected secret experiments.

The scout never forgot that odd foray up West Hill, or other encounters with the inventor who deeply impressed him and helped shape his own future career. As the sun dipped behind the horizon on that windswept hill, John Logie Baird took the wraps off a large, saucer-like metal dish with a spike in the centre, connected through a battery to a small receiver with a glass screen, which appeared to be covered in small metal particles. [...]

The most striking aspect of [the] story is the date. Baird was operating an object-detection apparatus with a screen at exactly the same time as he is thought to have stumbled on the inspiration to investigate his old enthusiasm, television. While there is little doubt that he made vital breakthroughs in Hastings, that town's true link with Baird could well be based, not on television, but on the birth of radar and other detection systems.

Baird himself would later add to the confusion about what he was really doing in Hastings. In his autobiographical notes and numerous newspaper features he describes how, in order to swell funds, he made a glass razor blade that would not rust or tarnish – and cut himself rather badly. He then turned to pneumatic shoes. Inside a pair of large boots he fitted two partly inflated balloons and set off on a trial run. He lurched uncontrollably for 100 yards, followed by a few delighted children; the episode ended when one of the 'tyres' burst. He continued:

> More thought was needed. I went for a long walk over the cliffs to Fairlight Glen, and my mind went back to my early work on television. Might there not be something in it now? My difficulty then had been to find a means of amplifying the infinitesimally small current from the selenium cell. Such an amplifier was available thanks to Britain's Ambrose Fleming and the American Lee De Forest. Why not try again? The more I thought of it the easier it seemed. I thought out a complete system and returned to Walton Crescent, with an influx of new life.

Descriptions of Baird's days at Hastings tend to depict him struggling. The financial hardship was real enough but 1923 saw Baird not, as often described, resident only in Hastings but also working on television 400 miles away, back in his home town, Helensburgh; and later in Folkestone, London and Tunbridge Wells. In Helensburgh he was seen working in a friend's outhouse, and an edition of the local newspaper of the time reveals that he had the cooperation of a wireless and electrical company, Youdall and Sprott of 78 West Princes Street. In Folkestone a plaque was later erected at 36 Guildhall Street following the revelation by a retired company director that Baird had experimented in 1923 on the premises of, and with the aid of, T.C. Gilbert & Co., an electrical contracting firm.

The various groups involved seem to have worked in total ignorance of Baird's experiments elsewhere. In Hastings he had brought his not inconsiderable powers of persuasion to bear upon a whole range of people who were fired up by his burning enthusiasm. Displaying the same talent for enlisting help from all walks of life that he had shown in the West Indies, he soon had a team of almost a dozen occasional assistants, all unpaid, eager to aid this extraordinary man of vision. They included Ronald Hartnell, a marine engineer who made a light chopper and discs; Vincent Edwards, a mechanical engineer with Hastings Tramways, who worked on some of the drive mechanisms; Norman Blackburn, a radio engineer; Boyd Alexander, a local radio enthusiast; George Farmer, who worked for a local undertaker and helped Baird with woodwork; a Mr Claude Froude; Norman Loxdale, the schoolboy who had helped him drag his apparatus up West Hill and who was also a radio ham; William le Queux, a prominent wireless enthusiast, journalist and author, who helped Baird generally, especially with publicity; a Mr Wells, a turner by trade; and a Mr Siddell, a chief engineer with the Post Office.

But perhaps the most significant presence was that of J.J. Denton, then an engineer with the municipal corporation of Hastings. This fascinating individual, twelve or more years older than Baird, was to work alongside him in a sort of freelance capacity until his own death in 1944. Other colleagues of Baird's never quite figured out Denton's role, but it is now clear that this staunch ally was one of the very few people who were privy to the inventor's secret aims. Denton was largely self-educated, but had shown such original talent that in 1895 he was accepted as a lecturer in physics at Morley College, London, with which he remained connected for the rest of his life. The two men met at Hastings through a common interest in a technical book available at the local library. Baird had tried to consult the book several times, without success, and one day asked the librarian when he might possibly obtain it. Pointing to Denton, the librarian replied: 'Ask him. That's the man who's got it.' At that meeting common ground was established and a lifelong alliance formed.

Another of the assorted band of helpers named by Norman Loxdale, one who played an outstanding role in the work at Hastings, was Victor Mills, by then a retired schoolteacher still living in Hastings. Mills gave Baird invaluable help with the selenium cell. They frequently disagreed, but it is clear that Baird respected the judgement of the young radio enthusiast.

Mills described Baird's recruiting methods in a 1978 newspaper article. The inventor had read reports of the sophisticated wireless set built by the schoolboy at Hastings Grammar School, as Mills then was. One day in February 1923 he turned up at Mr Mills' parents' home in Hughenden Road. Mrs Mills returned from the front door and told her son: 'There's a funny man at the door asking for you.' The schoolboy then encountered a figure in a long, soiled raincoat who explained he was trying to invent television.

Mr Mills wrote: 'I remember saying to him: "What's television?"

"Seeing by wireless," he replied. "You probably know something about resonance. I'm getting a picture but I can't do anything with it. I'm getting too much noise ..."'

By the 1930s cathode ray tubes and all-electronic systems were available for domestic television sets but Baird was ahead in mechanical television techniques including stereo, colour, outside broadcasts, recording video and even international transmissions. Many believe he advanced the growth of television by ten years.

By early 1925 Baird was trying to transmit the image of an object by reflecting light from it rather than by having a source of light behind the object. He said later:

The apparatus therefore has to be capable of detecting changes of light, probably at least a thousand times less in intensity than when shadowgraphs are being transmitted.

And he continued modestly:

The letter H for example, can be clearly transmitted, but the hand, moved in front of the transmitter, is reproduced only as a blurred outline. A face is exceptionally difficult to send with the experimental apparatus, but with careful focussing, a white oval, with dark patches for the eyes and mouth, appears at the receiving end and the mouth can be clearly seen opening and closing. The apparatus here demonstrated is, of course, absolutely 'in the rough' – the question of finance is always an important one for the inventor. But it does undoubtedly transmit an instantaneous picture. The picture is flickering and defective and at present only simple pictures can be sent successfully; but Edison's first phonograph rendered that 'Mary had a little lamb' in a way that only hearers who were 'in the secret' could understand and yet, from the first result has developed the gramophone of today ...

We should perhaps explain that we are in no way financially interested in this remarkable invention, the demonstrations are taking place here because we know that our friends will

Virginia Woolf.

Radclyffe Hall.

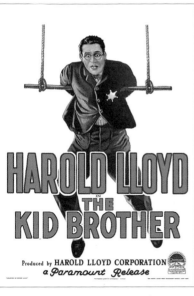

Poster for Harold Lloyd's 1927 film.

W. Somerset Maugham.

Buster Keaton and Marion Mack in *The General.*

Don Bradman is carried by teammates after scoring 452 not out for New South Wales.

Crowds gather at the premiere of *Don Juan* with John Barrymore.

John Logie Baird.

Ramsay MacDonald.

Actress Lilian Braithwaite with Noël Coward. They co-starred in his play, *The Vortex*.

A selection of Morris cars on a garage forecourt.

A publicity still from the film, *Journey's End*.

Cleaner sweeping the floor after the Wall Street crash of 1929.

be interested in something that should rank with the greatest inventions of the century.

There were few competitors to Baird in Britain in 1924 and 1925 and indeed, whenever television was mentioned in the press his name was always mentioned. Only he could give demonstrations of television equipment that showed the transmission of crude outlines. He would later describe his achievement in a radio broadcast in New York:

In 1925 television was still regarded as something of a myth. No true television had ever been shown – only crude shadows. At that time I was working very intensively in a small attic laboratory in the Soho district of London. Things were very black; my cash resources were almost exhausted [he was in fact down to his last £30, or £1,800 in today's money] and as, day by day, success seemed as far away as ever I began to wonder if general opinion was not after all, correct, and that television was in truth a myth. But one day – it was, in fact, the first Friday in October – I experienced the one great thrill which research work brought me. The dummy's head ... suddenly showed up on the screen not as a mere smudge of black and white, but as a real image with details and graduations of light and shade.

I was vastly excited and ran downstairs to obtain a living object. The first person to appear was the office boy from the floor below and he, rather reluctantly, consented to subject himself to the experiment. I placed him before the transmitter and went into the next room to see what the screen would show. The screen was entirely blank, and no effort of tuning would produce any result. Puzzled and very disappointed, I went back to the transmitter and there the cause of the failure became at once evident. The boy, scared by the intense white light, had backed away from the transmitter. In the excitement of the moment I gave him half a crown [12.5p, or £7.50 in today's money], and this kept his head in the right position. Going into the next room I saw his head on the screen quite clearly. It is curious to consider that the first person in the world to be on television should have required a bribe to accept the distinction.

Baird was now faced with a dilemma. He needed funds and therefore publicity but he was worried that television would be exploited by more powerful interests. He said later:

I was extremely nervous in case while I waited someone else achieved television – terrified that someone would copy my work, and particularly frightened that big wireless concerns would take up my television research and use my work as a guide.

The date chosen for the first public demonstration of television was Tuesday 26 January 1926. *The Times* reported it:

Members of the Royal Institution and other visitors to a laboratory in an upper room in Frith Street, Soho, on Tuesday saw a demonstration of apparatus invented by Mr J.L. Baird ... For the purpose of the demonstration the head of a ventriloquist's doll was manipulated as the image to be transmitted, though the human face was also reproduced. First on a receiver in the same room as the transmitter, and then on a portable receiver in another room, the visitors were shown recognisable reception of the movements of the dummy's head and of persons speaking. The image as transmitted was faint and blurred, but substantiated a claim that through the 'Televisor', as Mr Baird has named his apparatus, it is possible to transmit and reproduce instantly the details of movement, and such things as the play of expression on the face.

Baird also recorded his memories of the momentous day. He wrote, after noting that 40 members of the Royal Institution had accepted his invitation:

In one room was a large whirling disc, a most dangerous device, had they known it, liable to burst at any minute and hop around the room with showers of broken glass. However, all went well except for two small incidents. One of the visitors who was being transmitted had a long white beard, part of which flew into the wheel. Fortunately, he escaped with the loss of a certain amount of hair. He was a thorough sportsman and took the incident in good part and insisted on continuing the experiment and having his face transmitted. The whole assembly here were given an opportunity to be televised and I was certainly gratified by the interest and enthusiasm. The audience were, for the most part, men of vision and realised that in these tiny flickering images they were witnessing the birth of a great industry.

The equipment Baird had used was amazingly simple. There were 716 biscuit tins, bobbins, darning needles, cardboard from hat boxes, a pair of scissors, a few bicycle light lenses, a used tea chest, an electric fan motor and a variety of lenses. He had been seen going into antique shops and scrapyards looking for odds and ends such as Meccano parts.

That same year Baird, seeking publicity, went to the *Daily*

Express head office. The news editor was apparently terrified and one of his staff quoted him as saying:

> For God's sake, go down to reception and get rid of the lunatic who's down there. He says he's got a machine for seeing by wireless! Watch him – he may have a razor on him.

As Baird's friend Sydney Moseley would write in his book *John Baird*:

> Fame came to him, in fact, long before his too early death and there was a moment when a considerable fortune lay within his grasp. But he did not seize it. Whatever money he made – and by some standards he made a good deal – he expended chiefly upon the furtherance and the perfecting of his inventions.
>
> Yet in Britain he never gained the recognition which was his due, and to this day few of his compatriots realise that John Logie Baird ranks among the greatest inventors of this or any other age. It may be true that no one man can claim the whole credit for any epoch-making scientific advance. There are always many explorers crossing the frontiers of present knowledge into the dimly apprehended territory of inspired deduction. Baird, however, was to television what Marconi was to ordinary radio. That is to say, he outdistanced every other explorer in the field and established his country's claim to world priority in visual broadcasting.

Baird and the BBC

For some reason Baird and John, later Lord, Reith – the first director general of the BBC – never seemed to get on well.

Sydney Moseley explains the background in a chapter of his book *John Baird* entitled 'The monopoly says "no"':

'I met Reith for the first time,' [Baird] wrote, 'in rather unfavourable circumstances. I was always very short-sighted, and, at the beginning of one of the classes, the Professor asked if those who were short-sighted and wanted front seats would hand in their names. When I went up to the platform to hand in my own, three large, impressive young students were talking to him. They were talking on terms of equality.

'As I did so, the heaviest and most overpowering of the three "heavies" turned round and boomed at me: "Ha! What is the matter with you?"'

The heaviest of these 'heavies' was, of course, John Reith, later to be knighted and, later still, to be given a peerage. My friend, John Baird, was from the first over-awed by Reith's height, his apparently lofty social standing and his superb air of self-confidence.

It can be readily understood, therefore, that when Baird needed nothing so urgently as the BBC's co-operation, however limited, he found it well-nigh impossible to go direct to Reith and ask for his personal help.

Let there be no mistake about the fact that the successful development of Baird's system of television was dependent utterly upon the goodwill of those who controlled the broadcasting monopoly in Great Britain. Baird had made many successful transmissions and had given notable demonstrations of his inventions, and these had enabled him to raise very large sums of money from the public. But the hard fact remained that he could not make a commercial success of his invention unless the BBC allowed it to 'go on the air' or, most unlikely, television was granted an independent entity – which Baird preferred. [...]

Let it suffice, therefore, to say that the attitude of the BBC in regard to John's invention was precisely what might have been expected from a great monopoly suddenly confronted with an innovation which might conceivably force it to modify its entire programme and even to change its basic policy.

From the outset, therefore, the BBC displayed a stubborn reluctance to give Baird so much as the chance to prove his claims. Undeterred by this adamant opposition, I bombarded scientists, notabilities and politicians to come and see for themselves what Baird could do. I harangued Mr Lees-Smith, then Postmaster-General, in his room at the House of Commons for about an hour and a half. He listened with hardly an interruption, and in the end he shook my hand and just said: 'You've done a fine job!'

Then I went to see Sir Herbert (now Lord) Samuel, and was received with sympathy and understanding. He soon perceived the nature of Baird's dilemma and, as he remarked to me when we met again in October, 1951: 'It is not a happy position when any great monopoly can impede progress.' He felt strongly that Baird should be given a fair chance.

Moseley arranged for Baird and Reith to have a meeting but, although it was fairly cordial, the result was still unsatisfactory as far as Baird was concerned. As Moseley wrote:

It was not long, indeed, before this discouraging attitude hardened and the tragic situation became clear. In short, the BBC – through its Director-General and its chief engineer, Captain P.P. Eckersley – said one word to all propositions for BBC co-operation. That one word was: No. Whatever excuses could be made for this blank negative, its significance was deadly clear. The immense Baird Television Company, which had raised around £1,000,000 from a willing British public, was doomed to collapse without the co-operation of the one authority which had exclusive use of the air.

It was not long before I realized that there were powerful sections of opinion sceptical of Baird and his invention. A section of the technical Press supported the BBC's policy, despite the warm welcome given to Baird Television by the non-technical British Press. There can be no doubt that the feud between the BBC and the Baird Company, which was long, bitter and costly, could and should have been avoided. Much money and time which could otherwise have been expended profitably in the laboratory were dissipated in this stubborn struggle. [...]

[The BBC's] attitude was understandable enough up to a point, but need it have altogether prevented the Director-General from taking his humble, but brilliant compatriot under his wing in the early days?

Had he done so there might have been less need for Baird to have become so involved with Big Business and High Finance. As it was he was left with no choice. He had to make what friends he could in competitive business circles. Luckily for them, Lord Reith and his associates did not have to touch even the fringe of the world of finance. This was not because they had qualities which Baird lacked; it was merely because they lived in the shelter of the Corporation's secure monopoly.

CHAPTER 5

WILLIAM MORRIS – 'A FORD WITH AN OXFORD EDUCATION'

B y the time he was sixteen years old William Morris realised that his father, Frederick Morris, who had been suffering from ill health for a number of years, did not have much longer to live and that he would soon be the major breadwinner in the family.

He was an apprentice to a local cycle dealer and repairer, realised that he was underpaid and when his request for a pay rise of one shilling a week was refused he resigned. With a capital of four golden sovereigns (£400 in today's money), he set up his first workshop in a small brick shed in the garden of his parents' house, 16 James Street in Oxford. He soon needed more space and his parents allowed him to use the two front rooms of this terraced house as a store and showroom. When he outgrew this space too he rented his first shop at 48 High Street, Oxford. One of his first sales was to the well-built rector of St Clement's Church, and the daily sight of the large rector on his bicycle soon led to further sales.

An early contract was secured when the local head postmaster commissioned him to service and repair the bicycles used by the boys employed to deliver telegrams. His bicycle business flourished not only thanks to his hard work but also due to the fact that bicycles were popular in the university town of Oxford.

In 1899, realising that he wanted to expand beyond Oxford, Morris booked space at the annual cycle exhibition in London. John Minns, whose father married Alice, a sister of William Morris, wrote this of Morris's early days in business:

His ambition began to flourish and never left him, but it was an ambition to make vehicles not money. This preoccupation with severely practical objectives rather than any urge to get rich can be seen as one of the causes of his two very casually entered into partnerships which were soon to embarrass him financially. His single-minded aim was first to make the perfect cheap cycle, then a good motor cycle, and, much later, a good reliable car at a price affordable to the working man. The product was his sole ambition, not the means of making a rich reward for himself. His charges and prices were always very low, relying on the volume sales to prosper. His outlook was to the workshop as the instinctive priority for relentless energy, needing each day to achieve a better product than yesterday. Such a fixation gave scant attention to the growing need for financial backing and virtually none to his personal gain.

Even as his enterprises prospered in later years, surplus funds were ploughed back into further expansion as they were created. Wealth came to him in later years almost as a surprise but did not alter him significantly or his way of life.

As Morris's cycle business grew he expanded it into motorcycles as well and, to enable his business to grow, went into partnership with two others. However, this did not work and the company went bust. After this Morris resolved never to go into partnership. Furthermore, the number of motor cars that the wealthy undergraduates of Oxford brought him to service and repair made him realise that the future was the motor car.

He decided he must manufacture motor cars and one of his customers, the undergraduate Earl of Macclesfield, made him an unsecured loan of £4,000 (about £440,000 in today's money). Morris went to his banker, A.B. Gillett of Gilletts Bank, now Barclays Bank plc, in High Street,

Oxford. Audrey Taylor's book *Gilletts, Bankers of Oxford and Banbury* relates Gillett's account of the interview:

> Morris was in the bank asking to see me. He came with a scheme of his to assemble first class parts of a small car and was going to do the assembling. The money position came into it because I asked Morris what money he had got and he replied that Lord Macclesfield had lent him £4,000. I said to him, 'But how much have you got?' and he answered, 'A shilling' [5p, or £3 in today's money]. Then I said, 'Well, I will lend you another £4,000' and he looked at me in utter astonishment and said, 'Do you mean that?'. I replied that, 'My dear fellow, this thing you have told me about has got a fortune behind it.' Then I asked, 'How many cars are you going to make?' He said, 'Well, Mr Gillett, It is all a question of finance but we now have £8,000. Even so that is not too much for what we are going to do.'

1919

William Morris founded the company WRM Motors Ltd to build bullnose Morris cars before the First World War, and during the war stopped manufacturing cars to produce munitions.

However, in 1919 Morris put the company into liquidation and formed Morris Motors Ltd to take over its assets. The main reason for this was to allow Morris to rid himself of an onerous agency contract. In 1913 he had appointed a sole 'wholesale and shipping agent' for Morris cars for all areas outside London. This system did not allow extension of sales in the rest of the UK and overseas.

Morris was keen to expand and felt the compensation he had to pay to this agent was worthwhile. Production and sales rose steadily from a modest 387 in the whole of 1919 to 140 cars a month by April 1920. In July and September there were even 280 in each month.

However, the general downturn of 1920 was felt by Morris as well as many others and costs were rising. For example, Morris felt obliged to raise the price of his two-seater Morris Cowley from £315 (nearly £19,000 in today's money) in 1919 to £465 (nearly £28,000) in October 1920. This coincided with what became known as the biggest slump in the motor industry.

Morris Motors' sales fell as follows:

September 1920	276
October 1920	235
November 1920	137
December 1920	92
January 1921	74

Morris hoped the slump was temporary and still planned to increase production. However, in February 1921 he felt obliged to reduce sale prices. The four-seater Morris Cowley was cut by £100 to £425 and the two-seater by £90 to £375. He did at least persuade his distributors to take a cut in their commission from 17.5 to 15 per cent.

The price cuts worked. Here are the sales for the first six months of 1921:

January	74
February	236
March	400

April	361
May	352
June	361

Sales then fell away again and Morris reacted by cutting prices further.

The rest of the motor industry was shocked and many manufacturers gave up and went out of business. 1921 was a terrible year for the motor industry with production falling by a third to 40,000 vehicles, which was several thousand fewer than in 1913. However, Morris's output increased by over 50 per cent from 1,932 to 3,076 vehicles.

In 1922 output by Morris doubled to 6,956 cars, establishing the company as the leading motor car manufacturer in the UK.

Morris expanded his range. Even while Morris Motors concentrated on the 11.9 horse power (hp) Oxford and Cowley cars, it soon offered a bigger choice of specification in order to meet a greater variety of customers' requirements. Morris thus sought to develop to the full the demand for his type of car. Five models were listed altogether when the 1921–22 prices were advertised; the following season there were nine, including an all-weather Oxford and deluxe models of the Cowleys. The 1922–23 list is also notable for the inclusion of a sports car version of the Morris Cowley two-seater.

Together with this widening of the range of models, the specifications of the standard Oxfords and Cowleys were continually improved, and additional accessories and improvements were included as they were developed to the point where they could be produced inexpensively enough to be standardised in models intended for wide sale. Important changes were at first offered as standard 'extras'. Thus, in January 1922, the Morris Cowley cars were also offered with self-starters and extra dickey seats for ten guineas more than the models without these developments; but the more simple models continued to be produced until any such extra had been so established in public favour as to be thought essential equipment.

The Morris Cowleys of all types still provided the company with its 'bread and butter'. Although the prices of these were set as finely as possible, the policy remained to force down still further the costs and prices of all models as turnover expanded. We cannot continue to trace this development in detail, but we should mention the large reductions which occurred only one year after the first big price cuts. In 1922, competing manufacturers announced substantial reductions in prices for the following season. After these others had announced their new prices in readiness for the motor show, Morris kept his lead by cutting prices of all models then in production by amounts which varied from 20 to 35 guineas.

And the price cuts continued:

	Price on 2 November 1921		Price on 24 October 1922
	£	s	£
11.9 hp Morris Oxford			
two-seater	414	15	330
four-seater	446	5	355
two-seater coupé	483		390
chassis	304	10	220
11.9 hp Morris Cowley			
two-seater	299	5	225

four-seater	341	5	255
chassis	267	15	175

These prices need to be multiplied by 60 to give the prices in today's money so, for example, £414.15 is £24,849 while £175 is £10,500.

The effect of all this on sales per year was almost magical:

1918	204
1919	387
1920	1,932
1921	3,076
1922	6,956
1923	20,048
1924	32,918
1925	55,582

This meant that the Cowley factory in 1923 and 1924 was producing 28 per cent of the national output of this type of vehicle; in 1925 this rose to 41 per cent.

A journalist in the *Daily News* wrote on 21 November 1925:

I remember driving along the Bristol road from Birmingham some four years ago, when the chauffeur, commenting on the vehicles we met, said he estimated that 95 per cent of the cars normally on that road were Ford cars. If they were not flagrantly Ford, they were Fords in disguise. To-day on that road, as on any other road in the country, the overwhelming majority of cars that would be met would bear the signature of W.R. Morris. He has, as a witty friend of mine observed, given us 'a Ford with an Oxford education'.

Morris himself was not just an engineer but a brilliant businessman. This is what one of his employees said of him:

> His best asset was his nice appreciation of price and costs. Basically, he was a buyer and a very acute buyer indeed. Anything he bought, he bought at a very keen price, and he would get it in the end. The basis of Cowley is buying, not manufacture.

Another said:

> Morris always had second sight. He liked to think of himself as an engineer, but really he was a prince of commerce, because he had an instinct to know what the people wanted, to know what the next man was thinking, a buying capacity, and so on. Those gifts were much greater than his engineering ability, although that was not small.

This is what Morris himself said about prices when writing about his life and his business:

> I have said that one of the vital elements in securing success to-day is price. My aim is to keep ahead of the market. We have never waited for the public to ask for a reduction. We get in with the reduction first. Is it quite sufficiently realized in this country that every time you make a reduction, you drop down on what I may call the pyramid of consumption power to a wider base? Even a ten-pound price reduction drops you into an entirely new market. If the man cannot pay the last £10 ... he cannot buy the car ... The one object in life of many makers seems to be to make the thing the public cannot buy. The one object in my life has been to make the thing they can buy.

There is another current opinion that, if you only make enough of a given article, your price will come down dramatically. This is not the fact. To get bed-rock selling price you have to be practising every sort of economy, great and small, all the time. There are no marble halls at Cowley, and there never will be. Not an unnecessary penny is spent on selling or publicity. Every ha'-penny available is put into the production. So far this policy has justified [itself by] results. From 1912 to the end of 1918 I did not spend one shilling in advertising. The goods sold themselves. Even now, I rarely go outside the trade press. But to keep down costs you must have a staff of workers who are interested. My experience is that if you look after your men they will look after you.

Of his financial polices he wrote:

I have never gone to the public for ordinary capital. In consequence, all the directors are 'still under one hat'. This ... gives rapidity of action ... I can get things done while [a Board of Directors] would be brooding over them. For instance, I rang up the principal of a certain firm and proposed buying their factory one Wednesday morning. The following Friday afternoon I had bought the concern and completed the financial arrangements. Six weeks afterwards we were into production ...

My second financial policy is to demand payment promptly and to pay absolutely on the spot. A firm that is supplying us knows that whatever happens on the day which is arranged for our monthly payment our cheque will be in the office. The small manufacturer can budget accurately. He can save himself – and me – an enormous amount of money by being able himself to pay all his bills promptly. We are equally stern with others. As soon as we 'black-list' a customer we cut him off from supplies. I believe in facing financial facts; and the fact is that if you do not pay your bills promptly the other man assumes you have not got the money. He therefore determines to make an extra profit out of you to cover what he generally considers an extra risk. Finally, I believe in the budgeting of finances every week. The Secretary presents me with a weekly statement which actually shows the financial condition of the company at that moment.

And on the subject of sales:

Personally, I do not think that this country has yet really taken to motoring seriously. Until the worker goes to his factory by car, I shall not believe we have touched more than the fringe of the home market. So I have little fear for the disposal of our 35–50,000 cars this year!

The problem of our sales side is not so much finding the buyer – although it may come to that when our sales are many times their present volume – as discovering means of educating the retailer to our point of view which is – expansion ... The problem of our sales department is perhaps a little peculiar. In this country, the dealer has got into the habit of thinking of car sales in small numbers. Yet our whole aim is to sell cars in large numbers. We get our own profit; we keep the dealers' profit reasonable; simply in order that we may be able to sell cars in quantities. Having educated the dealer to this point of view, the next trouble of the sales manager is to train him to the idea of personal expansion. For instance, if one of our dealers sold a hundred cars last year, he was probably extremely pleased with the result. He thinks his show rooms, his sales staff and everything else is superb – and good for another ten years. What our sales department wants, however, is a sale of 200 cars next year and not a repetition of the previous feat. To get such a result, the commercial manager has not only to convince the dealer that the worry and trouble of expansion is worthwhile, but has to talk to him about better showrooms, about the cubic space arrangement for the sale of larger numbers of cars, of the art of selling and advertising, of the number of staff required per sale, and so on.

Two sales problems [are] common to most concerns to-day ... The one is undercutting, the other is complaints. Everything from railway locomotives to razor blades is subject to price cutting at the present time. Under conditions like these, nothing can prevent this. Perhaps we take more care than many others in the field, to catch out the miscreant.

Wherever we find that the price of a car has been cut below our standard rates, we hold the direct dealer who controls the territory in which the price cut was given absolutely responsible. The sales department takes the utmost trouble to discover precisely by whom the sale was carried through. Usually, it is some small dealer who is trying to favour a client. When we have traced down the dealer responsible, we insist on the payment of the difference between the price at which the car was sold and the list price. Practically every week we have a cheque in as a result of an illicit sale which we have tracked. We actually discovered one man who had sold a car for a profit of 10s. It frequently happens that a small dealer will be able to sell a £200 car for a profit of £5. When such a dealer gets squeezed out there can be little wonder. On such a basis the making of a sound net profit is impossible.

One continual source of anxiety to the owner is the cost of running repairs. A little garage in Cornwall may charge three times as much as a city garage for de-carbonizing, grinding in valves, and re-setting tappets – a process necessary to all cars, even the Rolls Royce. We are, therefore, instituting a system of standardized repair charges. One of the things we have to impress on the dealer is the necessity for holding a sufficient stock of spare parts. Only under these conditions can we give service to the owners of Morris cars. It will be realised that most of the work attached to dealing with complaints falls under the same heading – the giving of services to the man who had once bought the car. The satisfied customer is one of the best possible selling media in this trade – for motorists are incorrigible talkers of 'shop' … Only by service after purchase can you keep the owner satisfied – and get his selling force behind your product.

The MG

Morris Garages (MG) began to build the MG sports car at the beginning of the 1920s. By 1923 it was capable of a speed of 80 miles per hour and it was decided to offer it as a regular line. Initially the chassis, radiator and engine were the standard products of the Morris group. However, each car was individually 'hotted-up' for the specialist market. The engines were stripped down and carefully tuned to give maximum performance, the cylinder heads and ports were polished with the ports being enlarged; aluminium pistons, stronger valve springs and special magnetos, carburettor and exhaust manifolds were fitted and several other special components incorporated.

The car was so successful and sales grew to such an extent

that an MG factory was built at Cowley followed by another at Abingdon.

In 1928 the MG Midget was introduced. This car was intended to combine the characteristics of a sports car with the low upkeep and reliability of a low-priced touring car. MG cars generally were to become famous for their racing and competition successes. For example, the MG Midget was the first car of its class to go faster than 100 miles per hour and to cover 100 miles in one hour. By 1939 it held no fewer than seventeen records for cars under 750 cc.

In the 1920s Morris began to acquire companies. One of the first was Wrigleys, a maker of motor components and small tools. Morris had bought axles from them before the First World War but nothing after the war, and Wrigleys had collapsed and gone into liquidation. Morris bought the company from the receiver for £213,044 (about £13 million in today's money). The main attractions were Wrigleys' large factory and modern machining equipment. Under Morris, Wrigleys became Morris Commercial Cars Ltd.

Its first vehicle was the Morris one-ton truck and the first one was delivered in May 1924. Initially this new company made a loss but in the twelve months to May 1925 it made a profit of £39,000 (about £2.3 million today). Morris was now successfully launched into this new section of the motor vehicle market. At the higher end Morris Commercial also moved into taxi cabs and ambulances.

In addition, Morris wanted to expand in the export market and Morris Commercial management were encouraged to develop a car suitable for the conditions of the British Empire, especially Australia. Their first car was the 15.9 hp 'Empire Car' which was a powerful, roomy car which could travel over rough ground. It was not successful and many of the cars shipped to Australia had to be brought back. To try to increase exports generally, Morris then bought the French company Léon Bollée.

The Austin Motor Company

Sir Herbert Austin, who had founded and still ran the Austin Motor Company, wanted to merge with both Morris and Wolseley Motors and he arranged a meeting in London in May 1924 between himself, Morris and Dudley Docker, who represented Vickers which controlled Wolseley.

The meeting was short as Morris could not see the advantages which the other two saw. Nevertheless he asked them to send the papers embodying the proposal of a merger to his accountant. Morris rejected the proposal largely on the basis that it overvalued both Austin and Wolseley. Furthermore it wanted to transfer all production to its plant in Longbridge near Birmingham.

In the event Morris bought the Wolseley company but did not merge with Austin (that came much later).

His next purchase was the SU Carburettor Company which he bought in December 1926 for £100,000 (£6 million in today's money). The SU was short for 'Skinners' Union'; the two brothers who owned the company gave it the name as they both came from the family that owned the shoe firm Lilley & Skinner.

After the Second World War Morris Motors *did* merge with the Austin Motor Company. Morris had already been raised to the peerage as Lord Nuffield and he eventually retired as a director of the merged company, British Motor Corporation. He had been married since 1903 but there were no children to provide for, and so he made several very generous donations both to charities and to educational establishments such as Birmingham University. He also contributed to the founding of Nuffield College, Oxford. He died in August 1963 aged 85.

CHAPTER 6

RAMSAY MACDONALD – THE FIRST LABOUR GOVERNMENT

In January 1924 Ramsay MacDonald was sworn in as the first Labour prime minister. This was considered sensational by many, especially those in the upper and middle classes. Some feared that it might mean a Russian takeover, that property might be confiscated and marriage banned. Considering he was the illegitimate son of a farm labourer and a housemaid in the Scottish countryside it was truly remarkable.

Others wondered whether, when MacDonald and his senior ministers went to Buckingham Palace, they would wear top hats. As they waited for the King, a journalist noted that 'MacDonald, the starveling clerk, Thomas, the engine driver, Henderson, the foundry labourer and Clynes, the mill-hand, had all risen to this pinnacle!'

J.R. Clynes, the Labour party's leader in the House of Commons under MacDonald, noted how effectively the King put them at their ease, saying:

> I had expected to find him unbending. Instead he was kindness and sympathy itself. Before he gave us leave to go he made an appeal I have never forgotten: 'The immediate future of my people, their whole happiness, is in your hands, gentlemen. They depend on your prudence and sagacity.'

This is what MacDonald said in a speech on 13 February 1924:

> This country requires stimulation in its hopes; it requires to settle down to trade and development. It requires to be given courage and confidence, so that it may use its latent power; and above all, the common man and the common woman

must be brought into partnership of national prosperity. The unemployed, the partially employed, all must be taught that when we are talking of national greatness and prosperity, we mean them to be partners in that prosperity ... At this time of irrational timorousness – when pessimism and optimism are striving for mastery – I appeal to everybody, I appeal to the House, to go out with hope, to go out with determination, to go out not for tranquillity, but for security and confidence based on good will, and to be just and worthy of respect. In that spirit the Labour Party propose to act.

MacDonald was born in Lossiemouth in Morayshire, Scotland on 12 October 1866, the illegitimate son of John MacDonald, a farm labourer, and Anne Ramsey, a housemaid. He left school in 1881 at the age of fifteen and worked on a nearby farm. In 1885 he became an assistant to a clergyman in Bristol, Mordaunt Crofton, who was trying to establish a Boy's and Young Men's Guild at St Stephen's Church. He moved to London in 1886 and, after a period of unemployment, became an invoice clerk.

His interest in socialist principles was growing and he joined C.L. Fitzgerald's Socialists' Union. However, in the 1880s politics was of less interest to MacDonald than pursuing his education and he took evening classes in science, botany, agriculture, mathematics and physics at the Birkbeck Literary and Scientific Institution. In 1888 he became a private secretary to Thomas Lough, a tea merchant and radical politician who became the Liberal Member of Parliament for West Islington in 1892.

This opened doors into politics for MacDonald and he left Lough to become a freelance journalist. He also became a member of the Fabian Society.

The Fabian Society had been founded in January 1884 and its purpose was, and still is, to promote greater equality of power, wealth and opportunity; the value of collective action and public service; an accountable, tolerant and active democracy; citizenship, liberty and human rights; sustainable development; and multilateral international cooperation.

The Society soon attracted a number of prominent members of society such as George Bernard Shaw, H.G. Wells and Bertrand Russell as well as MacDonald, and at its core were Sidney and Beatrice Webb.

Many Fabians participated in the formation of the Labour party in 1900 and in the early years of the new century socialist ideas became more popular; the Fabian Society grew accordingly. Indeed, the Fabians lobbied for the introduction of the minimum wage in 1906, for the creation of a universal healthcare system in 1911 and for the abolition of hereditary peerages in 1917.

The Independent Labour Party (ILP) had been founded by Keir Hardie in 1893 and MacDonald successfully applied for membership in May 1894, being adopted as the candidate for a seat in Southampton. However, he suffered a heavy defeat in the election the following year. He stood again in the 1900 election, this time for a Leicester seat. However, he lost again.

In 1900 he also became secretary of the Labour Representation Committee (LRC), the forerunner of the Labour party, and he negotiated with the Liberal politician Herbert Gladstone, son of the late Liberal prime minister William Gladstone, a deal whereby Labour could contest a number of seats without Liberal opposition.

By coincidence he married Margaret Gladstone in 1896,

but she was not related to the Gladstones of the Liberal party. She was not wealthy but had enough resources for them to travel the world, going to the USA and Canada in 1897, South Africa in 1902, Australia and New Zealand in 1906 and India on several occasions.

Margaret proved to be a great asset to MacDonald. He said of her:

> To turn to her in stress and storm was like going into a sheltered haven where waters were at rest and smiling up into the face of heaven. Weary and worn, buffeted and discouraged, thinking of giving up the thankless strife and returning to my own house and children and household shrines, I would flee with her to my Buckinghamshire home and my lady would heal and soothe me with her cheery faith and steady conviction and send me forth to smite and be smitten. No one, not even I, can tell with accuracy how much of the steadiness that there is in the Labour movement of this country is due to her.

In 1906 the LRC changed its name to the Labour party, amalgamating with the ILP, and in that year MacDonald was elected MP for Leicester. By this time there were 29 Labour MPs, and MacDonald became one of the leaders of the party.

In 1910, Keir Hardie, founder of the Labour party, described MacDonald as 'the biggest intellectual asset that the Socialist Movement had'.

MacDonald wrote a number of books: *Socialism and Society* in 1905, *Socialism* in 1907, *Socialism and Government* in 1909, *The Socialist Movement* in 1911, *Syndicalism* in 1912 and *The Soviet Unrest* in 1913. In total they made a decisive contribution to the Labour party's thinking.

In 1911 he became party leader. However, his opposition to any sort of warfare meant that when war broke out in August 1914 he felt that he could not support the government's request for £100 million of war credits and resigned as party chairman; instead, he took the party treasurer's post.

For his opposition to Britain's involvement in warfare MacDonald became unpopular and was accused of treason and cowardice. Former Liberal MP and publisher Horatio Bottomley (see *Headline Britons 1921–1925*) attacked him in his magazine, *John Bull*.

He gradually regained his popularity but, nevertheless, lost his seat in the 1918 general election in which the Liberal David Lloyd George's coalition government won a large majority. Labour came out of the election with only 63 seats, which was an improvement on 1910 but hardly suggested that MacDonald would be prime minister within six years. Although MacDonald stood for parliament in the 1921 Woolwich East by-election he was not successful and it was only in the following year that he regained his seat when he won at Aberavon in Wales, and once again became party leader. Labour's magazine, *New Leader*, wrote:

> MacDonald's election is enough to transform our position in the House. We have once more a voice that must be heard.

And the historian Kenneth Morgan wrote:

> As dissolution set in with the Lloyd George coalition in 1921–22, and unemployment mounted, MacDonald stood out as the leader of a new kind of broad-based left. His opposition to the war had given him a new charisma. More than anyone else in public life, he symbolised peace and internationalism,

decency and social change ... [He] had become THE voice of conscience.

By 1922 the Liberals were in sharp decline and Labour under MacDonald became the main opposition to Stanley Baldwin's Conservative government. The next great event was the 1923 general election in which the Conservatives lost their overall majority. In January 1924, they lost a vote of confidence in the House of Commons and King George V asked MacDonald to form a Labour government with Liberal support. He was now not only the first Labour prime minister, but the first prime minister from a working-class background and one of the very few without a university education.

King George V wrote in his diary:

Today 23 years ago dear Grandma died. I wonder what she would have thought of a Labour Government!

In the 1924 election the free-trade sentiment was undisguised, and Labour increased its representation. 'We stand for free trade not because we think that free trade will solve any problems,' said MacDonald, 'but because we are not going to allow gentlemen interested in the land and monopoly capitalism to mislead us from the cures we intend to apply to the unemployed problem.' He also proposed that all work be done under good conditions and that the entire world should be seen as a potential market for British goods and services. He also believed that protectionism created new millionaires and sacrificed the true interests of the worker and consumers.

The result of the election was 257 seats for the Conservatives, 192 for Labour and 157 for the Liberals, meaning the Conservatives didn't have enough of a majority to form a government. The Liberals therefore held the balance of power and Asquith opted to support Labour rather than the discredited Conservatives. He said:

> If a Labour Government is ever to be tried in this country, as it will sooner or later, it could hardly be tried under safer conditions.

Harold Laski, a professor at the London School of Economics and eventually chairman of the Labour party in 1945–6, said of MacDonald in 1924:

> It is very exhilarating to watch the process of government from the inside ... I respect MacDonald more and more. It is, after all, a great thing to be prospectively the first Labour prime minister in English history; but he takes it with soberness and dignity and with a full sense of the arduous work involved. And he has a reading mind – the ethos of life means much to him. He sees the significance of things like research and enquiry, and he will use the non-political expert, I think, to a greater degree than ever before.

Marian McLeod, in her book *The Parliamentary Speaking of Ramsay MacDonald*, wrote of his ability:

> Ramsay MacDonald possessed and displayed several qualities which identified him as a leader. First, he exhibited that common sense that is much prized in British public life and which was the main characteristic of the Scottish school of philosophy; in fact, he seems to have had an uncommon share of common sense. Second, he was identified in the public

mind as an essentially optimistic person, and it is a truism that the politician who proffers the world hope rather than despair is welcomed at almost every door, while the pessimist is thought of as the apostle of a sterile and unproductive creed. Yet MacDonald's optimism was always circumscribed by an element of practicality – of common sense – so that never did he promise the unattainable [...] But he had confidence in the ability of ordinary British men and women to improve their own bailiwick [...] he took a characteristically British viewpoint and proclaimed the socialist future as a consequence of adherence to due process of law: he was ever the advocate of evolutionary change, of gradualism and propriety that some of his colleagues mistook for conservatism. In fact, his penchant for 'the idyllic peace of a quiet life' disposed him from time to time to see common cause with Conservatives rather with the raucous left-wing of the Labour Party.

MacDonald's outstanding intellectual attribute was, incontrovertibly, a keen and ordered mind that planned and supervised every task thoroughly and defined issues with uncommon clarity. [...] He apparently saw his responsibility as keeping the party together as a viable, effective one rather than to develop or elaborate upon theory. Ever the pragmatist, he constantly reminded his party that none of their goals could be realised unless the party gained and maintained political power.

MacDonald's personality was such that he was often encouraged to proceed alone, and his naturally introspective or even taciturn disposition (combined with a somewhat aloof or patrician mien) made many feel that he was reluctant to share his thoughts and feelings with others. This hypersensitivity and reticence are not traits usually found in politicians, and his reserve partly accounted for the distrust that he encountered from other Labourites. [...] This same element of style is discernible in much of his written work: [...] only occasionally does he rise to flights of emotional power, only rarely does he allow his fundamentally gentle, sympathetic, and warm self to surface.

Undoubtedly MacDonald put the welfare of his party and of the nation ahead of his personal interests.

This is a book about the period 1926–1930 highlighting its interesting personalities of which Ramsay MacDonald was one, but to understand MacDonald's behaviour in that period we need to summarise the period in 1924 when he was prime minister of the first Labour government.

On 19 January of that year, MacDonald had written: 'Sometimes feel I should like to run away home to Lossie to return to reality & flee from these unreal dreams. I am a Socialist because I prize above all things the simple life & here I am in this, encountering it on the way to Socialism ... So I swing between my two beings and go on.' Three days later he was prime minister at the age of 57.

Labour was to show it could rule responsibly. MacDonald's government dealt with a series of strikes and instituted some reform in the area of domestic social policy. Philip Snowden would show himself to be a reliable and conventional chancellor and parliamentary business depended upon Liberal and sometimes Conservative cooperation. Foreign affairs took up much of MacDonald's time and, in the context of Versailles, he was instrumental in securing the withdrawal of the French from the Ruhr. The Labour government also recognised Soviet Russia but subsequent draft treaties unnerved the Conservatives and the Liberals.

In the end, though, this first Labour government was to be

short-lived. The collapse of the government was precipitated by its failure to prosecute a British Communist, and in the election that followed, MacDonald mishandled the 'Zinoviev letter' affair. Labour lost many parliamentary seats – but not votes – in October 1924 and, within days, the party was back in opposition.

When Labour were defeated and out of power at the end of 1924, Harold Laski, mentioned above and also one of MacDonald's loyal supporters, wrote to him:

> At first sight the vista of the next five years appears unendurable. But I do want you to feel that historically this is a necessary prelude to the greater drama ... People who have become accustomed to the epoch of Lloyd George cannot immediately make the transition to the epoch of Ramsay MacDonald. But have faith. Realise that we all care deeply about you, that we have confidence and hope because you stand erectly by us.

MacDonald and the General Strike

As we have seen, in 1925 the mine owners proposed to end the existing wage agreement and, in spite of almost continuous negotiations which, at times, included the Conservative government, a general strike – the first in British history – began on 3 May 1926.

On 4 May 1.5 million workers came out on strike, as well as printers, some building workers and those in heavy industry and gas and electricity supply. After another week they were joined by engineering and shipbuilding workers. The TUC closed down all newspapers.

MacDonald's involvement was confined to a speech in parliament. He did not believe in general strikes and later described them as 'clumsy and ineffectual', saying:

If the wonderful unity of the Strike which impressed the whole world with the solidarity of British Labour would be shown in politics, Labour could solve mining and similar difficulties through the ballot box.

The General Strike was called off on 13 May but the miners remained locked out of their mines. MacDonald became involved in taking the miners' leaders to an informal meeting with the chancellor of the exchequer, Winston Churchill.

The General Strike was an important event for both MacDonald and the Labour party. To begin with, coal had been a dominant part of British industry for over 100 years and had been the country's biggest export. However, its contribution slumped in the 1920s, partly because Germany's reparations to France and other countries, ordered by the Treaty of Versailles, were paid in coal from the Ruhr valley. Furthermore, when France and Belgium moved into the Ruhr valley the harmful effect was felt by the British coal industry.

When the General Strike broke out MacDonald called for moderation by both owners and miners and talked of the strike as a 'calamity' and 'great suicidal fight'. He became more convinced than he was before that socialist thought would evolve in England through education and legislation rather than confrontation. He felt that socialism should succeed through economic strength and national unity, not from distress and decline.

While in opposition from 1925 to 1929 MacDonald did mix with friends outside the political arena. He began looking for a new residence in the Regent's Park and Hampstead area within a month of leaving office. His per annum salary of £400 (£24,000 in today's money) as MP had recently been improved by a legacy left to him by H.H. Markwald, his benefactor, who died while MacDonald was in office. Markwald had supported him and other Labour politicians with insurance accounts and educational and other funds for their children. MacDonald saw no harm in this charity. Markwald lived in Switzerland and sought no favours and MacDonald had always accepted gifts from others with no intention of paying them back in kind or with favours. When Markwald's will was made public, however, there were some who worried the right-leaning press would use it against MacDonald.

With the Markwald legacy and other support, which may have included a loan or gift from biscuit manufacturer and philanthropist Alexander Grant, MacDonald bought a house in Upper Frognal in Hampstead Heath. It was secluded and spacious – a physical expression of his desire to set himself apart again to write and contemplate.

Some people may have thought the house and district a bit too smart for a Labour politician, but MacDonald himself was comfortable with it and it allowed him to cultivate more friends outside the world of politics.

Visitors included a variety of literary, artistic and other professional people who discussed a wide range of topics. Scotsmen such as John Buchan, Alexander Grant and John Barrie visited frequently at Upper Frognal. Leading physician Thomas Horder also became a close friend, both because medicine and science were two of MacDonald's favourite topics and because he often passed along gossip from his well-placed Conservative and Liberal patients.

Alexander Grant, now a peer, remained his best friend. The Grant family lived only a few miles east of Lossiemouth on the Moray coast and the families saw a great deal of each other on holidays. MacDonald persuaded Grant to finance several Scottish projects, such as the Scottish National Gallery and the National Library of Scotland.

MacDonald may have felt that life after Downing Street would be more settled and contemplative, but he was wrong. To meet expenses, he made speeches and wrote commissioned articles. He complained he had to write on Sundays and scurry around for other sources of income, but then he had always been worried about money. This concern did not prevent him from purchasing furniture and art work, sending his children to private schools, and travelling. He went to the West Indies in December 1924, spent seven weeks in Ceylon the next year, journeyed to North Africa in 1926, and visited the United States in 1927. He also maintained a full-time secretary, Rose Rosenberg, who kept his correspondence and writing organised.

Even so, he continually protested that he experienced no relief and was obliged for financial reasons to maintain a schedule of mind-numbing work that was becoming 'impossible almost & means incessant drudgery with no rest, no gaiety, no lilt in life. I cannot go on, & yet what can I do? I am like a man wading in a river with the water up to his neck & not knowing but that the next step will take him out of his depth.' Asthma and bronchitis attacks made him irritable and wore him down. In a prophetic passage of self-diagnosis, he wrote that if this type of work 'killed one in a clean, efficient business-like way why should one object, but it cripples & tortures first by lowering the quality of work done & then pushing one into long months of slowly ebbing vitality & mental paralysis.'

That spring of 1927, Ramsay and his daughter, Ishbel, sailed to the United States for a lecture tour. He had learned from experience that these tours could be highly successful for British political figures. He had many American friends and truly enjoyed visiting the States.

The 1929 election

As the general election of 1929 approached, the Liberal party were determined to regain the position they had surrendered to the Labour party during the 1920s. Lloyd George decided to concentrate on the major issue of the day, unemployment. He adopted the slogan 'We Can Conquer Unemployment.'

MacDonald tried to portray the Liberals as a spent force. He had already written in 1922: 'When parties outlive their historical period, the magnetism goes out with them ... Is not this the history of the Liberal Party since the death of Gladstone?' Parliament was dissolved on 10 May 1929 and the election took place three weeks later.

While Labour's manifesto – or as they called it their 'Appeal to the Nation' – included the usual promises of slum clearance, new roads, electrification and land drainage, it did contain some significant changes such as calling for the nationalisation of mine and mineral royalties, raising the school leaving age to fifteen, improved pensions, a commitment to free secondary schools, pensions for widows and orphans, and export credits to stimulate depressed economic areas.

MacDonald ran an inspired national campaign. He wisely undercut the Conservative vote by insisting that a change in government was needed. He largely played down the above manifesto, and by doing so he secured Conservative voters who instinctively distrusted Lloyd George and were left uninspired by their own party's manifesto and dull slogan, 'Safety First'. MacDonald also wooed the Liberal vote, reasoning that Lloyd George's programme to solve unemployment would be considered too radical by many.

The Labour party secured 288 seats in the new House of Commons against the Conservatives' 260 and Liberals' 59. Again, as in 1924, a combined Conservative and Liberal vote might have prevented Labour from taking office, but neither opposition party risked it. Baldwin left without fanfare, and MacDonald formed his second Labour government.

The Liberals had increased their representation, but only to 59. The composition of the parliamentary Labour party had also changed significantly. The number of MPs sponsored by local Labour parties had increased five-fold, to 128. The 115 trade-union-supported members were, for the first time, not a majority. The ILP had won 36 seats and the Cooperative party nine. MacDonald was the undoubted victor but, if he was to form a second Labour government, he would still be dependent on the Liberals.

One of the first things MacDonald did in his second term as prime minister was to organise a visit to the United States. On 28 September 1929, shortly after he had been re-elected as prime minister, he sailed for the United States, where Wall Street was about to suffer its great crash which triggered the depression of the 1930s. He sailed with his daughter Ishbel in the German vessel *Berengaria* which had originally been designed for Kaiser Wilhelm.

It was a successful trip, thanks largely to the fact that he understood Americans better than any of his predecessors and the Americans loved him.

The editor of the *New York Times* wrote:

> His bearing has been perfect. Not one slip in act or speech did he make while he was here. Deeply impressive has been his abiding sense of high mission on which he came and which he hopes will lead to all embracing benefits throughout the entire world. His eloquence has been that of elevation of mind and nobility of purpose.

The general view among Americans of British parliamentarians was that they were reserved and stuffy, but MacDonald's charm and pretentiousness won them over. This had an important effect on relationships between the two countries in the difficult two decades to come.

He returned on 1 November and the editor of the *Observer,* James Garvin, wrote to him saying:

> No Prime Minister since the separation in 1783 has done anything like your solid and lasting work for Anglo-American settlement.

Directly after his return he went to see his new friend, Lady Londonderry (his wife had died of blood poisoning in 1911). Many felt that this friendship with a noblewoman would limit MacDonald's enactment of extreme socialism.

Looking at the years 1924–29, this is what David Thomson wrote of them in his *England in the Twentieth Century*:

> The first Labour Government, headed by MacDonald, took office in January 1924. The second, also led by MacDonald,

took office in June 1929. The time between these two events was a strange interlude in British national life and in Britain's internal and Commonwealth relations. After the phase of anguished settlement and aftermath which ended in the gloom of 1923, these years came as a time of hope and promise. The waste land, it seemed, had at last been traversed. The most outstanding features of the new landscape were, in economic life, a growing prosperity despite persistent mass unemployment; in politics, a mood of conciliation and pacification marred by the General Strike of 1926; in external relations, an era of better feeling and firmer cooperation, of efforts to establish good relations with Germany and the Soviet Union, marred by outbursts of animosity. [...]

[Conservative prime minister Baldwin's resignation] happened on 21 January 1924, and the next day MacDonald ... became Prime Minister [...] The need for Liberal support in order to survive precluded any specifically socialist legislation. So did the sheer inexperience of the Labour ministers. The Prime Minister had no previous ministerial experience at all. Among his colleagues, only Henderson and Haldane had previously been in a Cabinet. [...]

The ministry was to last only nine months, and the 'next step' was not to come until 1929. Meanwhile Labour in office contributed in two important ways to the new mood of hopefulness which began to prevail. In home affairs it tackled housing and unemployment – the two social evils that were undoubtedly the most urgent: in foreign affairs MacDonald, as his own Foreign Secretary, pursued a policy of pacification. [...]

[The] housing shortage remained acute, prices high, the building trades disorganized; and Chamberlain's small subsidized houses were condemned as 'rabbit hutches'. Wheatley and his able Parliamentary Secretary, Arthur Greenwood, tackled the housing problem imaginatively and with vigour. They prepared a programme to produce 2½ million houses by 1939. The Housing Act eventually became law in August 1924. It was the main domestic achievement of the first Labour Government.

Unemployment proved a more intractable problem. Though figures of unemployed had fallen far below the peak of May 1921, they seemed to have stabilized at over 1 million. In 1924 it was still hoped to reduce this figure drastically, especially in those 'distressed areas' where industries in deep slump meant very high local figures of unemployed. In 1924 the need for more generous poor relief was met by extending unemployment benefits and by amending the Insurance Acts in several ways. Payments went up from twelve to fifteen shillings a week [60p to 75p, or £36 to £45 in today's money] for women, from fifteen to eighteen for men, and the children's allowance was doubled to two shillings. [...]

In foreign affairs it was a similar record of partial achievement and partial frustration. One aim was to get on to good terms with the Soviet Union. Normal diplomatic relations, severed since 1918, were restored in February. Then came negotiations about trade and finance, and treaties were signed in August. At the same time MacDonald agreed to the Dawes Plan for settling the vexed question of German reparations, still bedevilling Britain's relations with France and Germany alike. It was over its relations with Communism that the Labour Party fell from power in October, and lost its majority in November.

When Labour won the election in 1929 and MacDonald

was again prime minister, they had won on the basis of the heavy unemployment among the working class. By the mid-1920s the post-Great War period of prosperity was over. Unemployment rose to over 2 million, with the north of England and Wales particularly badly affected. The National Unemployed Workers' Movement (NUWM) organised a hunger march from the north-west to London in both 1928 and 1930 but they were shunned by the Labour party, refused an audience with MacDonald and even run down by mounted police in London.

MacDonald now had to govern faced with the realities of the economic situation and not on the basis of ideals. Unfortunately, he was soon faced with a world economic crisis brought about by the collapse of shares on Wall Street in the autumn of 1929. The economic depression between 1929 and 1932 reduced world trade by no less than two thirds, as well as being instrumental in the seizure of power by Adolf Hitler's Nazi party in Germany. Unemployment in the UK rose to 2 million in 1930 and nearly 3 million by Easter 1931. MacDonald, dependent as he was on Liberal Party votes, could not cope and he was forced out of power.

He died while on a sea voyage with his daughter in 1937.

CHAPTER 7

NOËL COWARD

B everley Nichols, the famous author and composer, once said:

> And then there was the sound of laughter outside, and in walked Noël Coward, and whenever Noël walks into a room the spotlights automatically switch towards him.

Noël Coward was born in Teddington in south-west London on 16 December 1899 and, acquiring his ambition from his mother, began his professional work at the age of only ten as Prince Mussel in the children's play *The Goldfish*. Coward himself wrote this in his memoirs:

> One day ... a little advertisement appeared in the *Daily Mirror*. It stated that a talented boy of attractive appearance was required by a Miss Lila Field to appear in her production of an all-children fairy play, *The Goldfish*. This seemed to dispose of all argument. I was a talented boy, God knows, and, when washed and smarmed down a bit, passably attractive. There appeared to be no earthly reason why Miss Lila Field shouldn't jump at me, and we both believed that she would be a fool indeed to miss such a magnificent opportunity.

He continued to act in his teenage years and during the First World War. In 1917 he appeared in a comedy, *The Saving Grace* by the actor-manager Charles Hawtrey. Coward would say later:

> My part was reasonably large and I was really quite good in it, owing to the kindness and care of Hawtrey's direction. He

took endless trouble with me ... and taught me during those two short weeks many technical points of comedy acting which I use to this day.

Coward began to write plays himself and, in 1920, he starred in his own comedy, *I'll Leave it to You*. It first appeared in Manchester but then moved to the New Theatre in London (renamed the Noël Coward Theatre in 2006).

Reviews were mixed. The *Manchester Guardian* was a little grudging and the *Observer* wrote:

Mr Coward ... has a sense of comedy, and, if he can overcome a tendency to smartness, he will probably produce a good play one of these days.

However, *The Times* was more enthusiastic:

It is a remarkable piece of work from so young a head – spontaneous, light, and always 'brainy'.

Following some more plays and an educational trip to New York where he found the Broadway theatre 'stimulating', Coward achieved his first great success as a writer, *The Vortex*. On 16 December 1924 *The Vortex* opened at the Royalty Theatre with the author in the starring role. It was enthusiastically received and 25-year-old Coward celebrated by buying new suits, pyjamas, dressing gowns and silk shirts. Among those who did not care for the play was veteran actor Sir Gerald du Maurier. 'The public are asking for filth', he declared. 'The younger generation are knocking at the door of the dustbin.'

Coward appreciated the value of publicity from an early stage in his career and was quite happy to be portrayed as a dissolute playboy. By 1925 he was acclaimed as one of the 'bright young things' bringing joy to a war-weary nation. Furthermore, his stylish way of dressing made him a trendsetter in men's fashion.

There were attempts to censor both novels and plays in the 1920s; in 1922 James Joyce published *Ulysses* in Paris as it was banned in Britain. In 1926 Coward's comedy *This Was a Man*, in which all the characters were adulterers, was censored by the Lord Chancellor and, consequently, the play was performed in New York, Berlin and Paris but not in Britain. As we have seen, Radclyffe Hall's *The Well of Loneliness* also had its circulation restricted.

In *We Danced All Night*, Martin Pugh describes the way *The Vortex* caught the mood of its time:

> In *The Vortex* Coward neatly caught the atmosphere of hedonism and decadence so typical of smart metropolitan society in the 1920s; his characters frequently appeared in dressing gowns and called each other 'darling'. The story revolved around a middle-aged woman enjoying an affair with a much younger man who took cocaine, a habit often interpreted as a mask for homosexuality at this time. It is not clear how the play escaped the attentions of the Lord Chancellor, and it was noticeable that in the [1928] film version all morally offensive aspects had been toned down, creating a bland reproduction of Coward's original.

The Vortex struck the right note for the 1920s and the characters were recognisable – the older woman, a war widow, who has a younger man as a lover, and her son who takes drugs. There is also a handsome guards officer who is good at games but not at anything else.

However, the story is about an over-sexed socialite and her drug-addicted son (played by Coward) and indeed, as we have seen, some people saw the drugs as a stand-in for homosexuality. It attracted large audiences and the Lord Chamberlain's office considered banning the play. Lord Cromer, the Lord Chamberlain, said:

> This sort of play is unfortunately the inevitable sequence to a play like *Our Betters* [a Somerset Maugham play which ran from 1923 to 1925 and caused a great scandal, though it got past the censors] by which it is evidently inspired. This picture of a frivolous and degenerate set of people gives a wholly false impression of Society life and to my mind the time has come to put a stop to the harmful influence of such pictures on the stage.

Even King George V was opposed to it, as Lord Stamfordham, the King's private secretary, announced:

> The King has read the papers and says evidently it is a disgusting play but, unfortunately, cannot be prohibited.

Others approved of the play. For example, Sir Anthony Havelock-Allan, later a prolific and successful film producer, said:

> Among the smart rich people, the café society, everybody took drugs ... it was very prevalent in the theatre. It was an English version of what happened in Paris after the war, when very rich American women came to find the gay life, and many had boyfriends young enough to be their sons ... That was the world after the horror of the First World War,

frenetic gaiety, stimulated and hopped-up with drink and drugs ... They were part of his world, those people.

The play was not banned and moved to the Royalty theatre in the West End on 16 December 1924. It certainly improved Coward's prosperity and promoted Coward himself. Cecil Beaton, the successful photographer, said:

> In the whole new spirit of affection and frivolity, the influence of the theatre was far from negligible ... It became a fad to talk with equal authority on specialised subjects as well as frivolous ones, to mingle cocktail chatter about great personages and events in history with jazz slang ... Men enjoyed imitating the exaggerated, clipped manner of certain leading actors and adopted the confident manner of those who are aware of their charms ... Noël Coward's influence spread even to the outposts of Rickmansworth and Poona (the city of Pune in India called Poona by the British in the nineteenth century). Hearty naval commanders or jolly colonels acquired the 'camp' manners of calling everything from Joan of Arc to Merlin 'lots of fun', and the adjective 'terribly' peppered every sentence.

The Vortex was also a success in New York where tickets were soon exchanging hands at double their face value. However, one critic claimed that the play would convince Americans that English society was completely decadent. Coward challenged this saying:

> You know perfectly well, and I presume everyone does, that the percentage of rotters in society is very small. In London today, despite the fact that the war left a great many people

groping, shattered mentally and morally, without any beliefs left in anything that gives them a moral anchor to windward, fashionable society as a whole is as sound and healthy as it has ever been.

He followed up his success with *The Vortex* with a succession of memorable productions including *Fallen Angels* and *Hay Fever* in 1925, *Bitter Sweet* in 1929, *Private Lives* in 1930, *Cavalcade* in 1931 and *Design for Living* in 1933.

As Martin Pugh notes:

Coward deliberately cultivated a reputation as an elegant, languid and slightly camp young man; he took a flippant view of moral and sexual questions and fed the newspapers with provocative observations. 'I am never out of the opium dens', he told the *Evening Standard*, 'My mind is a mass of corruption.' ... [His] writing betrayed considerable care and shrewdness. He mitigated the impact of his plots with witty dialogue, effectively making his audience laugh before it had time to be outraged; and although he freely included homosexuals in his plays, he did not follow Radclyffe Hall in writing about homosexual love. ... In time patriotism became an increasingly important element in his work. Beyond this, his appeal lay in his simple, melodious songs, many of which entered into popular culture of the time: 'I'll See You Again', 'Poor Little Rich Girl', 'Mad Dogs and Englishmen', 'The Stately Homes of England' and 'Don't Put Your Daughter on the Stage Mrs Worthington'. In these songs Coward faithfully reflected English sentimentality and a capacity for poking fun at the English without forfeiting his claims to patriotism. His work offered English audiences a suggestion of the risqué and the fashionable combined with the reassurance of conventionality. He was the authentic voice of the interwar period.

At the end of April 1925, Noël Coward's *Fallen Angels* opened at the Globe Theatre with husky-voiced Tallulah Bankhead in one of the leading roles. The play was immediately described as 'vulgar, obscene and degenerate' and became the talk of London.

On 29 August, the last night of the run, notorious public prosecutor Mrs Charles Hornibrook visited the theatre. This old lady had recently parted company with the London Council for the Promotion of Public Morality and was operating on her own. At the end of the second act, she stood up in her box. 'Ladies and Gentlemen, I wish to protest. This play should not go unchallenged.' In the disturbance that followed, there were hoots from the gallery, the orchestra struck up with 'I Want To Be Happy' and Mrs Hornibrook was gently guided out of the theatre.

The following day, the King and Queen attended Noël Coward's patriotic new musical *Cavalcade* at the Theatre Royal, Drury Lane. During the second interval, the author was presented to the King and a rumour flashed around the auditorium that he had been knighted, there and then, in the royal box.

While in the USA Coward became more friendly with the American Jack Wilson, who had been introduced to him by a mutual friend. They became close and Wilson gave up being a stockbroker to become Coward's personal manager. When they returned to England, Coward, by now a rich man, took Wilson on what was effectively a 'honeymoon' to France, as well as Sicily and Tunis which were two places popular at the time with wealthy young homosexual men.

During the 1920s, although homosexuals ran the risk of blackmail and even imprisonment, they found no difficulty in finding partners, especially in both houses and hotels in London. There were many famous men who pursued same-sex relationships including Harold Nicholson, Stephen Spender, Christopher Isherwood, Siegfried Sassoon and E.M. Forster. Somerset Maugham was promiscuously homosexual but he accepted the conventional advice of the time to live in France.

Coward had had his first relationship with another man when he was only fourteen and thereafter enjoyed a number of affairs, especially with actors such as Louis Hayward and Alan Webb. He also had what he called a 'little dalliance' with Prince George, the Duke of Kent, from 1923 to 1925. The prince was nothing if not adventurous; he indulged in alcohol and cocaine and was openly bisexual, favouring black women and young men.

By June 1925 Coward had no fewer than four shows playing in the West End – *The Vortex, Fallen Angels, Hay Fever* and *On with the Dance*. The *Observer* wrote this on 14 June 1925:

Mr Noël Coward has brought off his first real theatrical coup. *Hay Fever* is so good a comedy that description can say little about it.

He carried on producing for the rest of the 1920s and suffered only one real failure, *Sirocco*, which was about free love among the wealthy. Ivor Novello, the famous actor and composer, starred in it, moving Coward to write: 'The most two beautiful things in the world are Ivor's profile and my mind.'

However, many in the audience strongly disliked it, booing in the intervals and abusing, even spitting on Coward as he left the theatre. He would say later:

My first instinct was to leave England immediately, but this seemed too craven a move, and also too gratifying to my enemies, whose numbers had by then swollen in our minds to practically the entire population of the British Isles.

Coward did not announce publicly that he was homosexual; he was aware of the fate of Oscar Wilde a generation earlier and was nervous about the possibility of blackmail. Furthermore, he felt he and his friends should be discreet.

Roy Hattersley, in his book *Borrowed Time*, wrote:

The theatre was, in its own way, a dream factory. But between the wars it tackled subjects which the cinema would not have dared examine. And it dealt with them in a way which the bright young things of the period accepted as daring rather than dull. Noël Coward's *The Vortex* led the vogue for entertainment dealing with topics which were previously not discussed in polite society. The subject's sensational impact on West End audiences was increased by the suspicion that [main character] Nicky Lancaster – drug addict, 'up in the air effeminate' and consumed by affection for his promiscuous mother – represented attributes which, to a lesser degree, Coward shared. The young John Gielgud – chosen to play the part in America because he could play the piano! – described his lines as 'so extraordinarily characteristic that when you had heard [Coward] deliver them himself, it is almost impossible to speak them on stage without giving a poor imitation'. Neither the plot nor the characters made *The Vortex* a twentieth-century *Oedipus Rex*. But it did make audiences think – although the pleasure it provided to those who liked to shock the easily shockable was, in its way, an escape from the more prosaic problems of everyday life.

Coward had sufficient theatrical ingenuity to enable him also to play a part in providing the more conventional forms of escapism. Between the wars much of it was set to music.

Much of Coward's success was the result of his ability to judge the mood of the times. So he moved on from the risqué examination of social scandals to uninhibited nostalgia and romance. *The Vortex* and *Private Lives* – a frivolous examination of divorce and adultery – gave way to *Bitter Sweet*, a romance of Old Vienna. But it was America, not Europe, which colonised the popular theatre, as it was colonising the cinema.

By this time the 1920s was labelled 'the Gay Twenties', the era of the 'bright, young things', and this side of the era was portrayed in not only the comedies of Noël Coward but also the novels of F. Scott Fitzgerald and Evelyn Waugh.

Coward also befriended Radclyffe Hall and although it was not his style to give public support to Hall's *The Well of Loneliness*, he invited Hall and her lover, Una Troubridge, to visit him at his house in Aldington, near Rye in Sussex.

Sally Cline, in her biography of Radclyffe Hall, *A Woman called John*, wrote of Noël Coward:

Noël Coward and two friends turned up at The Black Boy for lunch. Una [Troubridge] revelled in showing them round and discovering that Noël 'adored every inch of the house'. He told tall stories so that they 'all howled with laughter', Una describing it as 'harmless and not ill-natured laughter such as Noël excels in. He is one of the only people ... who succeeds in being chronically and excruciatingly witty without victimising anyone or making anyone feel that his next excess will be at one's own expense.'

More conventionally, he was also friendly with Marie Stopes, the birth control pioneer, who wrote to a friend:

> The truth is out! and a young man [Noël Coward] 'spotted' me so I have had interesting talks all day. He is a dear and a dramatist and full of youth and enthusiasm and yet *sanity*. We agree absolutely about Aristocracy and he thinks you tremendously handsome and he is using his money success to help his mother and family and he is hoping to use his power of laughter to help in social progress and he told the people at my table that I am one of the greatest intellects which made them sit up ... I'm hungry for intelligent youth. Leatherhead is too grown up.
>
> I have read two of the plays of this interesting young author-actor – one is *very* good and one very bad – I told him it was 'putrid' and he took it ever so nicely ... I think he is not only *real* but was sent by Providence to re-open my interest in my dear old love, the drama.

Coward, though he later refused her offer to rewrite *The Vortex* with a focus on birth control, was sufficiently intrigued to send her a poem:

> If through a mist of awful fears
> Your mind in anguish gropes
> Dry up your panic-stricken tears
> And fly to Marie Stopes.

After Coward's death in Jamaica in 1973, he received deserved praise in his obituary:

> Posterity may reject his musicals as limited by the tastes and

techniques of the 1920s and 1930s. His serious pieces – like *Cavalcade* among his musicals, *The Vortex* and *This Happy Breed* among his plays – may seem too easily sentimental to appeal to later ages, but they reflect the mood of their times with startling clarity. Of all of his multifarious achievements, it is as a master of the comedy of manners that he is irreplaceable; his work in this special field is precisely written and, elegantly economical, it belongs to the classical tradition of Congreve, Sheridan, Wilde and Shaw.

He made his first great success with *The Vortex*, a somewhat melodramatic confrontation between a foolish, amorous, middle-aged woman and the drug-taking Hamlet who was her son. In it, Coward found an authentic desperation in the self-conscious gaiety of the first post-war period.

Hay Fever, written in a weekend in 1925, is a more dazzling achievement; like *The Importance of Being Earnest*, it is pure comedy with no mission but to delight, and it depends purely on the interplay of characters, not upon elaborate comic machinery. This was followed by a series of musicals produced by C.B. Cochran, which culminated in *Bitter Sweet*, probably the best of Coward's work for the musical stage, in 1929, and *Cavalcade*, a magnificently spectacular pageant of English history, from the death of Queen Victoria to the great slump, as it was seen through the eyes of an upper-middle-class family. *Cavalcade*'s sincere, sentimental patriotism converted to Coward's cause many theatre-goers who had distrusted the flippancy, the facility, and the witty light-heartedness of his earlier work. Between the two musicals came *Private Lives*, a comedy as beautifully and smoothly made as *Hay Fever*, and no less witty but with a closer relevance to the moral concerns of the day. It exploits with inventive delight its author's gift for retort discourteous, the comic inflation of the obvious, the urgent pursuit of the wild irrelevancy, and his mastery of cleverly economic effect.

Noël Coward was very adept at making brief but succinct comments on his way of life and that of those around him. Some of his most famous include:

I like long walks, especially when taken by people who annoy me.

Work hard, do the best you can, don't ever lose faith in yourself and take no notice of what other people say about you.

You ask my advice about acting? Speak clearly, don't bump into the furniture and if you must have motivation, think of your pay packet on Friday.

It's discouraging to think how many people are shocked by honesty and how few by deceit.

Thousands of people have talent. I might as well congratulate you for having eyes in your head. The one and only thing that counts is: Do you have staying power?

Mad dogs and Englishmen go out in the midday sun.
The Japanese don't care to
The Chinese wouldn't dare to
The Hindus and Argentines sleep firmly from twelve to one
But Englishmen detest a siesta.

Work is more fun than fun.

People are wrong when they say opera is not what it used to be. It is what it used to be. That's what's wrong with it.

Never trust a man with short legs. His brain's too near his bottom.

The stately homes of England, how beautiful they stand, to prove the upper classes have still the upper hand.

Wit ought to be a glorious treat like caviar. Never spread it about like marmalade.

Extraordinary how potent cheap music is.

I love criticism just so long as it's unqualified praise.

I've sometimes thought of marrying – and then I've thought again.

I am not a heavy drinker. I can sometimes go for hours without touching a drop.

I don't believe in astrology. The only stars I can blame for my failures are those that walk about on the stage.

I'll go through life either first class or third, but never in second.

Let's drink to the spirit of gallantry and courage that made a strange Heaven out of unbelievable Hell, and let's drink to the hope that one day this country of ours, which we love so much, will find dignity and greatness and peace again.

My body has certainly wandered a good deal, but I have an uneasy suspicion that my mind has not wandered enough.

Ever since a child of tender age the world has been a stage for me to dance upon; wedding bells would never ring for me, the only thing for me was 'getting on'.

CHAPTER 8

W. SOMERSET MAUGHAM

Like Noël Coward, W. Somerset Maugham was the source of many quotable aphorisms. Examples include:

No man in his heart is quite so cynical as a well-bred woman.

Imagination grows by exercise and, contrary to common belief, is more powerful in the mature than in the young.

The common idea that success spoils people by making them vain, egotistical and self-complacent is erroneous; on the contrary, it makes them, for the most part, humble, tolerant and kind. Failure makes people cruel and bitter.

At a dinner party one should eat wisely but not too well, and talk well but not too wisely.

I'll give you my opinion of the human race in a nutshell. Their heart's in the right place, but their head is a thoroughly inefficient organ.

Dying is a very dull, dreary affair. And my advice to you is to have nothing whatsoever to do with it.

It is not true that suffering ennobles the character; happiness does that sometimes, but suffering, for the most part, makes men petty and vindictive.

Hypocrisy is the most difficult and nerve-racking vice that any man can pursue; it needs an unceasing vigilance and a rare detachment of spirit. It cannot, like adultery or gluttony, be practised at spare moments; it is a whole-time job.

From the earliest times the old have rubbed it into the young that they are wiser than they, and before the young had discovered what nonsense this was they were old too, and it profited them to carry on the imposture.

You can't learn too soon that the most useful thing about a principle is that it can always be sacrificed to expediency.

A woman will always sacrifice herself if you give her the opportunity. It is her favourite form of self-indulgence.

Impropriety is the soul of wit.

A woman can forgive a man for the harm he does her, but she can never forgive him for the sacrifices he makes on her account.

Like all weak men he laid an exaggerated stress on not changing one's mind.

People ask you for criticism, but they only want praise.

Money is like a sixth sense without which you cannot make a complete use of the other five.

Few misfortunes can befall a boy which bring worse consequences than to have a really affectionate mother.

Drama enjoyed a heyday in the 1920s and was dominated by playwrights such as George Bernard Shaw and Somerset

Maugham. Huge crowds were drawn to the theatres in the West End and the 'Mad Hatters', a high society group around Elizabeth Bowes-Lyon (later married to the Duke of York, who became King George VI when King Edward VIII abdicated in 1936), wrote to each other constantly and rapturously about shows they had seen.

Maugham, born in 1874, had quite a difficult childhood. He lost both his parents by the time he was ten and was raised by an uncle who lacked warmth. Both his father and his grandfather had been successful lawyers and it was assumed that Somerset and his elder brothers would follow in their footsteps. Indeed, his elder brother, Viscount Maugham, did so and was appointed Lord Chancellor in 1938.

However, Somerset did not want to be a lawyer and he trained and qualified as a physician. But his real skills lay in the literary arena and his first novel *Liza of Lambeth*, published in 1897, sold so well that he abandoned medicine and became a full-time author. As he said later: 'I took to it as a duck takes to water.'

Even so, it took another ten years, during which his novels failed to repeat the success of *Liza of Lambeth*, before he enjoyed his next success with the play *Lady Frederick*. By the following year, 1908, Maugham had four plays running in London. Indeed, *Punch* published a cartoon showing Shakespeare biting his fingernails nervously.

By the time of the outbreak of the First World War in July–August 1914 Maugham had become well known thanks to his ten novels and ten plays. During the war he served in France as a member of the British Red Cross but continued to write, including the novel *Of Human Bondage*. This received both criticism and praise but is still in print in 2017.

Many believe that *Of Human Bondage* is Maugham's best

book. Its main character is Philip Carey who, like Maugham himself, is orphaned and brought up by a pious, even rather cold, uncle. While the real-life Maugham had a stutter which caused him constant embarrassment, he gave Carey a club foot which had the same effect.

Although many said it was an autobiography, Maugham himself said:

> This is a novel, not an autobiography; though much of it is autobiographical, more is pure invention.

Maugham's interest in art is also echoed by Carey. Maugham had in his collection work by four artists mentioned in the book: Pissarro, Sisley, Monet and Renoir. The book has been made into a successful film three times in the last 100 years.

During the war Maugham, although he was homosexual, began an affair with Syrie Wellcome, the wife of Henry Wellcome. Wellcome, an American by birth, had founded the company Burroughs Wellcome in 1880. He moved to Britain and in the twentieth century Burroughs Wellcome became one of the country's leading pharmaceutical companies. In 1995 it merged with Glaxo, and GlaxoSmithKline is now *the* leading British pharmaceutical company.

Wellcome and Syrie had married in 1901 but separated in 1909, and were divorced in 1917 after she had a child with Somerset Maugham in 1915.

Maugham and Syrie married in May 1917. This was also an unhappy marriage, particularly because Maugham was having an affair with his male friend Gerald Haxton. Finally, Syrie divorced Somerset in 1929. It cost Maugham his house in London with all its contents, his Rolls Royce and £2,400 (about £150,000 in today's money) a year, as well as £600 a year for their daughter, Liza.

By the second half of the 1920s Maugham had become one of the best known and most successful writer of plays, novels and travel books in Britain.

He had begun his many visits to the Pacific Islands in 1917 and this brought about some of his most successful novels such as *The Moon and Sixpence*, based on the life of the artist Gauguin, published in 1919. He also wrote travel books such as *On the Chinese Screen*, published in 1923, and *The Gentleman in the Parlour*, published in 1930, as well as several collections of short stories.

In 1928 Maugham published *Ashenden*, a group of short stories based on his own experience as an espionage agent during the First World War. Ian Fleming, the author of the famous James Bond books, said later that he was influenced by *Ashenden*.

By 1927, Maugham's close relationship with Gerald Haxton was causing him both embarrassment and fear of prosecution and he moved to France. He bought a villa in a property of nine acres at Cap Ferrat, which is between Nice and Monte Carlo, on the French Riviera. At his villa, called 'Mauresque', he lived a life of luxury though he continued to write. Members of the literary and social elite were delighted to receive invitations to spend time with him there. Maugham would famously describe the French Riviera as 'a sunny place for shady people' but he lived there for the rest of his life, and his tax status meant that he could not visit Britain for more than 90 days a year.

On his trips to New York, Maugham met Charlie Chaplin and they went to the theatre together where Chaplin was greeted with acclaim by the audience. Maugham thought how wonderful that must be. He was not entirely unknown himself by the mid-1920s and Ray Long, the fiction editor of *Cosmopolitan*, offered him a contract for eight stories at $2,500 a story. Maugham accepted, remembering as he did so a time when he had lived for two years on $2,500.

By the mid-1920s Maugham was also coming to the attention of foreign critics, as many of his books and plays had been translated into several languages. Indeed, the French regarded him as one of their own, a disciple of Maupassant and Flaubert. They hailed him as 'the Kipling of the Pacific' and 'the British Maupassant'. He was placed alongside Joseph Conrad, Robert Louis Stevenson and Edgar Allan Poe.

By the second half of the 1920s many successful English and American authors and playwrights had moved to the French Riviera. There was an Edith Cowell Avenue in Beaulieu, a Scotch Tea Shop in Nice and tea shops in Monte Carlo where customers could read the *Illustrated London News*. James Barrie and Michael Arlen were in Cannes, Frank Harris in Nice, H.G. Wells in Grasse, E. Phillips Oppenheim in Cagne, Edith Wharton in Hyères and, as we have seen, Maugham joined them in Cap Ferrat in 1927.

Following Maugham's divorce by his wife Syrie in 1929 – largely because of his affair with Gerald Haxton – Maugham had a further homosexual relationship with Alan Searle, whom he had met in 1928. He was good looking but was brought up in the London slum area of Bermondsey. One of Maugham's friends said of Searle: 'Gerald was vintage, Alan was *vin ordinaire*.'

Although Maugham's love life and his family relationships were fraught – he was not only divorced but fell out with his only daughter – he was nonetheless financially successful thanks to good book sales, successful theatrical productions and film adaptations, and some smart stock market investments. During the 1930s he wrote some well-received travel books and after the Second World War he set up the Somerset Maugham Award, which was given to the best British writer under the age of 35 for a work of fiction published that year. Winners have included V.S. Naipaul, Kingsley Amis, Martin Amis and Thom Gunn.

In 1954 Maugham was created a Companion of Honour but he was modest about his own achievements, describing himself as 'in the very first row of the second-raters'.

Perhaps his most famous quotes are:

> It's a funny thing about life; if you refuse to accept anything but the best, you very often get it.

> There are three rules for writing a novel. Unfortunately, no one knows what they are.

> The ability to quote is a serviceable substitute for wit.

Having been born in 1874 (the same year as Winston Churchill), he died in 1965 (also the same year as Winston Churchill).

CHAPTER 9

LOOKING TO THE FUTURE

As we have seen, the second half of the 1920s saw the heyday of many important and colourful characters in British public life. However, there were also two events of great national and international significance that occurred in this period, both of which would have implications that would last for decades to come. They were the extension of the right to vote to all British women in 1928, and the Wall Street crash of 1929.

All women have the vote

On the future of women's position in the electorate when women under 30 finally gained the right to vote via the so-called 'Flapper Vote Bill' in 1928, the *Observer* wrote:

WOMEN AND THE FUTURE

On 29 March 1928 universal adult suffrage was at last achieved in this country.

Under ordinary forms in the British way one of the extraordinary revolutions in democratic history has been ensured. In spite of the romantic resistance of a corporal's guard in the No lobby, the supremacy of a male electorate in this country was virtually abolished last Thursday by an overwhelming majority of male votes. The result will be to enlarge the electorate to the total of 26,000,000 voters, amongst whom women-citizens to the extent of a couple of millions will outnumber the men.

Ultimately some woman pre-eminent as orator and leader will become Prime Minister. If women have been great as queens and empresses, why not some day as Prime Minister? The experiment is bound to be proposed before the end of the twentieth century.

(It did happen, but not for 50 years!)

The introduction of universal suffrage is remarkable as terminating one of the longest and greatest processes in our own political history. The movement now completed has lasted for over a century and a half. The Duke of Richmond advocated manhood suffrage as far back as 1780. Looking back, the astonishing thing about the measure called The Great Reform Bill is that it made only the smallest and safest of changes. Even in 1867 Household Franchise only introduced a very limited democracy. That Act added about a million voters to the register. Still less than one tenth of the people were citizens. There was a bigger change in 1884 when the vote was extended to the agricultural labourer. Then, in 1918, women's suffrage made the tremendous increase. The electorate at one sweep was enlarged from about eight millions to over twenty millions.

The critics of this historic measure protest against it on the ground that it gives a permanent majority to women. On any basis whatever of equal rights women would still be a majority in politics just as they are in national life – though a majority not combined as a sex, in the manner once feared by egregious pessimists, but distributed amongst the three parties and differing from each other like men.

The Wall Street crash of 1929

As we have seen, the 1920s was generally a decade of economic stability and growth as Britain and the rest of the world recovered from the war years. This was especially so in the United States where the New York stock market boomed. Even working men were determined to get in on the act and it seemed as if millions bought shares, often with borrowed money. Actually it was only about a million people, but they made so much noise about making money that it seemed like millions. And many industries benefited. For example, car ownership in the USA rose from 8 million in 1920 to 23 million by the end of the 1920s. President Hoover said in 1928: 'We are nearer today to the ideal of the abolition of poverty and fear ... than ever before in any land.'

Of course, it could not last and, after two hiccups in March and May 1929, the New York market finally crashed on 29 October 1929, which became known as Black Tuesday. And this time there was no quick recovery. After a small recovery in April 1930 shares kept plunging so that, by the middle of 1932, the average industrial share was only worth 15 per cent of its 1929 value. The Dow Jones index took until 1954, or 25 years, to recover to the level it reached in 1929.

A few canny rich people escaped. The billionaire Rockefeller is supposed to have told his chief clerk a week before the crash: 'Sell everything we have.' When the clerk objected, Rockefeller replied, 'I've just heard two boot-blacks discussing stocks. Who's going to buy from them? Sell!'

Furthermore, because the effect of the crash on nearly all economies of the world was severe, a world depression began which would last for most of the 1930s. It will be covered in the next book in this series of *Headline Britons.*

INDEX